CHAKRAS OF MANAGEMENT

Ashutosh Garg worked in the corporate sector for twenty-five years before becoming an entrepreneur and founding the extremely popular Guardian Pharmacy chain in 2003. He also served as director of GAVI, the Vaccine Alliance (headquartered in Geneva), for eight years and has been a member of several other prestigious boards. Recognized as a Global Leader for Tomorrow by the World Economic Forum in 1995, he is an active member of the Young Presidents' Organization, the world's largest leadership community, and a charter member of TiE or The Indus Entrepreneurs.

He launched the popular global podcast 'The Brand Called You' (www.tbcy.in) in 2019 and has written nine highly acclaimed books, including some bestsellers, and can frequently be seen on national television discussing current affairs. A keen golfer, he also plays the Indian flute and enjoys reading.

Connect with the author at:
https://www.instagram.com/ashutoshgarg56/
https://twitter.com/gargashutosh
https://in.linkedin.com/in/coach-ashutoshgarg/

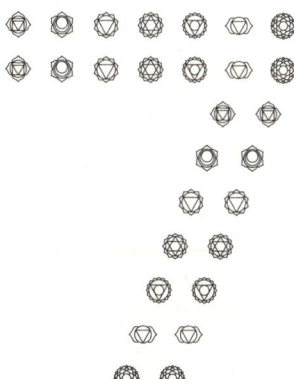

CHAKRAS OF MANAGEMENT
WISDOM FROM INDIC SCRIPTURES

ASHUTOSH GARG

Published by
Rupa Publications India Pvt. Ltd 2024
7/16, Ansari Road, Daryaganj
New Delhi 110002

Sales centres:
Bengaluru Chennai
Hyderabad Jaipur Kathmandu
Kolkata Mumbai Prayagraj

Copyright © Ashutosh Garg 2024

First published in Hardback in 2024
Published in Paperback in 2024

The views and opinions expressed in this book are the author's own and the facts are as reported by him, which have been verified to the extent possible, and the publishers are not in any way liable for the same.

All rights reserved.
No part of this publication may be reproduced, transmitted or stored in a retrieval system, in any form or by any means, electronic, mechanical, photocopying, recording or otherwise, without the prior permission of the publisher.

P-ISBN: 978-93-5702-679-6
E-ISBN: 978-93-5702-926-1

First impression 2024

10 9 8 7 6 5 4 3 2 1

The moral right of the author has been asserted.

Printed in India

This book is sold subject to the condition that it shall not, by way of trade or otherwise, be lent, resold, hired out or otherwise circulated, without the publisher's prior consent, in any form of binding or cover other than that in which it is published.

Dedicated to

our granddaughter
Vaani

my mother
Sudha Garg
who narrated countless stories from our scriptures to me

my father
Brig ML Garg, AVSM, Kirti Chakra

my wife
Vera

our sons
Varun and Ashwin

and

our daughters-in-law
Sakshi and Jody

∞

CONTENTS

Introduction ix

PART ONE

MULADHARA CHAKRA 3
Laying the Foundation, Creating Something New

SVADHISTHANA CHAKRA 26
Invoking Shakti, Infusing Energy

MANIPURA CHAKRA 54
Courage and Mental Resolve

ANAHATA CHAKRA 84
Emotional Intelligence and Accountability

VISHUDDHI CHAKRA 118
Connecting the Dots with Stakeholders

AJNA CHAKRA 155
Holistic Communication and Awareness

SAHASRARA CHAKRA 187
Connecting Businesses with the People

Management Chakras 221

PART TWO

The Vedas	231
The Bhagavad Gita	242
The Ramayana	252
Ancient Wisdom	265
Acknowledgements	270

INTRODUCTION

I started my career first as a professional manager for 25 years and then as an entrepreneur for the next 16 years. Throughout this journey, what kept me company were the stories (and the lessons derived from them) that I had heard in my childhood, narrated by four storytellers—my mother, my *nani* (maternal grandmother), my *babaji* (paternal grandfather) and an elderly caretaker and cook in my *nani's* house, whom we fondly referred to as *Panditji*. Whenever faced with uncertainty, I would search within for this reserve of knowledge and lessons.

It was only after I stopped working on a full-time basis that I started thinking of sharing this veritable treasure trove of knowledge contained in our scriptures—from the *Ramayana* to the *Mahabharata*, from the *Gita* to Chanakya's *Arthashastra* and *Chanakya Niti* and from the Vedas to the Upanishads. Whenever I was confronted with a challenge and wanted a different perspective on my professional and entrepreneurial journey, I went back to these stories (and continue to do so) for advice and inspiration. Soon, a pattern of the Seven Chakras started emerging in everything I had done until now.

I noticed that these Chakras transcended the scriptures

and even religion. They emerged from my basic understanding of our major scriptures as well as Sikhism, Jainism and Buddhism. Each of these three religions, originating from India, has their own scriptures and lessons, and is therefore referred to as Indic religions. I have also drawn on some lessons from Chanakya, Osho and Jiddu Krishnamurti.

I grew up believing 'Work is Worship' and asked my past self the reasons for that. I soon realized that the reasons were my mother, nani, babaji and Panditji, who regaled me with stories from the ancient Hindu scriptures. There was a new story or a continuation of an existing story at the dinner table every evening, narrated by my mother. With my grandparents, it was during our annual visits; their stories always concluded with important life lessons that stayed with me.

With Panditji, it was when we were seated on the floor in the kitchen while he cooked our meals. His animated stories, where he enacted his narration in between making the food, remain deeply etched in my mind. He was an amazing storyteller and knew exactly when to stop a story, leaving us on the knife's edge of excitement. We would wait anxiously through the following day, standing outside the kitchen, waiting for him to start cooking so that the next part of the story would be 'served' to us.

THE ORIGIN OF THE CHAKRAS

Chakras refer to the different focal points used in several ancient meditation practices. There is no unanimity on the number of Chakras because, over the years, the concept evolved and was interpreted differently by various sects, schools of thought and spiritual traditions within Hinduism.

In this way, Hinduism is internally diverse due to its inherent ability to accept multiple points of view; it tolerates dissonance in its interpretation by everyone in the manner they choose and it does not proscribe a single text that must be followed. Hindus can thus choose whether or not to follow any form of worship and even then they can continue to be 'good' Hindus.

As such, Hinduism, as a way of life, is constantly adapting to time and geography, and all believers in the Hindu way of life interpret and implement their own understanding of the beliefs. These beliefs change across the world while still following the underlying principles of worship. As far as the concept of Chakras is concerned, several sects within Hinduism have interpreted and understood it in their own unique way.

Hinduism will thus continue to evolve because Hindus are liberal and accept reality without any unnecessary dogmas. Even as a religion, the believers of Hinduism can question what they do not understand.

In fact, Hindu religious texts have helped most Hindus to develop boundaries and norms for living, holding themselves accountable and being responsible members of any community. These texts also provide Hindus with a set of anchors they can identify with.

The Vedic people believed that there was one Creator who manifested His form through various forms of nature, from the sun to the snow-covered mountains and the sea. In Vedic philosophy (Vedas are considered the oldest scriptures of Hinduism), *Hiranyagarbha*, meaning the golden womb, is believed to be the source of the creation of the entire universe.

As a practicing Hindu, I agree with this description of creation.

Creation has similarly been defined in other religious texts. What I learnt was the many ways in which the verses attempt to define the creator and then ask the simple question, 'What God shall we adore with our oblation?' These words helped me understand that I have a choice and can pray to any form I like because the ultimate creator is the same.

SHRUTI AND SMRITI

We have often heard the saying, 'a little knowledge is a dangerous thing', since it first appeared in Alexander Pope's *An Essay on Criticism* in 1709. Over time, we tend to become arrogant in the belief that we know everything and that there is nothing else to learn. I have always believed that there is something to learn from every interaction, irrespective of who the other person is.

Similarly, every time one reads the scriptures, they are bound to find something new. The number of years Hinduism has existed varies vastly. For my book, I will work with a more conservative age of between 5,000 and 6,000 years.

It is believed that there was a time when there were only Hindus on the whole earth. During an excavation in Mexico, ancient idols of Ganesh and Lakshmi were discovered. A 6,000-year-old Shiva temple was found in Africa. Statues of Vishnu, Rama and Hanuman have been found in ancient temples in China, Indonesia, Malaysia, Laos and Japan.

Hindu scriptures have been passed down through generations, whether through written text, referred to as

Shruti, or through memory, referred to as *Smriti*.

Shruti

That which has been heard or communicated from the beginning of time.

It is believed that the Vedas, considered to be the oldest text for Hindus, were received from the *Parambrahma* or *Parmeshvara* by rishis while meditating. Therefore, these are referred to as *Apaurusheya* (not of a person), meaning these were not created by human beings. The Vedas are believed to be the only scriptures that have been heard from the divine *Brahman*.

The word Brahman has two meanings in our scriptures. The commonly understood meaning is that a Brahman is a member of the highest Hindu caste, originally that of the priesthood. The deeper meaning is the Ultimate Reality underlying all phenomena in the Hindu scriptures.

The difference between the above two is with respect to pronunciation. Phonetically, the second one is pronounced as '*Brahmaan*' ('Ultimate Reality' or 'Consciousness' or 'Atman') and I will use this 'Brahman' in my book unless I state otherwise.

Coming back to the Vedas, it has been derived from the root *vid* (to know). The Vedas are also referred to as the books of knowledge, which talk about the nature of reality, i.e. 'what is this all about'. There are four Vedas:

- *Rig Veda*
- *Sama Veda*
- *Yajur Veda*
- *Atharva Veda*

Briefly, the *Rig Veda* contains hymns about our mythologies, the *Sama Veda* consists of hymns about religious rituals, the *Yajur Veda* comprises instructions for religious rituals, whereas the *Atharva Veda* embodies spells against enemies, sorcerers and diseases. Numerous lessons are contained within each of these but for the purpose of this book, I will restrict myself to the lessons that I have learnt.

Smriti

That which is remembered or based upon memory.

In other words, Smriti refers to that which originates from the human intellect. Smriti addresses our life problems, those that we encounter while following our dharma. Some of the important Smritis are:

- Bhagavad Gita
- Manusmriti
- Upanishads
- Ramayana
- Mahabharata
- Puranas

THE SEVEN CHAKRAS

While the number of Chakras may not be definite, the Seven Chakra System is commonly followed, consisting of six major chakras and a seventh point or centre known as the *Sahasrara* (the highest spiritual centre—pure consciousness—containing neither object nor subject).

The *Muladhara* or the Root Chakra is often referred to as the 'grounding' chakra, as it is associated with our connection to the Earth. A balanced root chakra provides a sense of stability and security, helping us feel grounded in life.

The *Svadhisthana* or the Sacral Chakra is strongly connected to creativity. A balanced sacral chakra contributes to emotional stability, healthy expression of feelings and the ability to form positive relationships as well as maintain them.

The *Manipura* or the Solar Plexus Chakra is associated with willpower and determination. A balanced solar plexus chakra encourages emotional resilience and the ability to manage stress effectively.

The *Anahata* or the Heart Chakra is closely linked to relationships, emphasizing healthy connections and harmonious interactions. A balanced heart chakra encourages mutual understanding, trust and support in both personal and social relationships.

The *Vishuddhi* or the Throat Chakra involves practices that promote clear and authentic communication. A balanced throat chakra advances effective communication by fostering the ability to listen attentively and empathetically.

The *Ajna* or the Third-Eye Chakra is associated with heightened awareness and expanded perception. A balanced third-eye chakra encourages an awareness of non-verbal cues, body language and the energetic undercurrents in communication.

The *Sahasrara* or the Crown Chakra connects us with a higher state of consciousness and fosters a sense of unity with the Divine and the Universe. A balanced crown chakra encourages us to recognize our place in the grander scheme of existence and appreciate the vastness of the cosmos.

In this book, I will use episodes from Indic religions to demonstrate the above-mentioned Chakras and how they can transform your life in the same manner they changed mine. All our scriptures are full of stories that explain how to live life. Most of these stories that we relate to are remembered and passed on to the next generation.

Storytelling is a powerful form of communication, evident in almost every aspect of our lives. So instead of long essays and sermons on management, I use storytelling, which results in two amazing things as these stories are retold every time. First, the storyteller adds their unique perspectives and experiences to their narratives. Second, the listener interprets the story based on their own understanding. And when the listener becomes the storyteller, life comes full circle.

WISDOM FROM INDIC SCRIPTURES

When I started thinking about writing this book, one of my big realizations came from a quote by Adi Shankaracharya (taken from Advaita Vedanta):

ब्रह्म सत्यं जगन्मिथ्या जीवो ब्रह्मैव नापर:।

This Sanskrit phrase, which is the essence of our scriptures, consists of two parts:

- *Brahma satya jagat mithya,* meaning Brahman (the Ultimate Reality) is real while the world is illusory.
- *Jivo brahmaiva naparah,* meaning the individual soul is non-different from Brahman.

Thus, most things and experiences in this world can only give temporary and not permanent happiness.

Verse 34 of Chapter 2 of the *Bhagavad Gita* is important in this context.

अकीर्तिं चापि भूतानि कथयिष्यन्ति तेऽव्ययाम्।
सम्भावितस्य चाकीर्तिर्मरणादतिरिच्यते।।

The above translates to 'we must do our duty and complete what is expected of us. We cannot neglect our work, which can lead to a loss of reputation. Disgrace comes when we neglect our duty or when we do an unrighteous deed. Disgrace is worse than death, for death destroys the body, but disgrace stains our fair name or reputation for generations.'

In the context of this book, I would then highlight to every reader that as we continue to aspire to achieve more in our personal and professional lives, we will encounter highs and lows, but we must always remember the bigger reality. We thus need to learn by studying and understanding ourselves, making our mind calm and directing our focus and concentration inward because learning never stops.

To that effect, the former President of India Dr Radhakrishnan states that at the core of all historical religions, there are fundamental types of spiritual experience, though they are expressed with different degrees of clarity.

But the subject of Hindu scriptures is vast, and it is impossible for me to try and cover even a fraction of the incredible amount of knowledge that exists within them. For this book, I have limited myself to a few of the better-known and popular ones. As I try to understand more from our scriptures, I may be motivated to write again in the future!

I have taken the liberty of assuming Sanatan Dharma as interchangeable with Hinduism. Purists may not agree with my assumption and I seek their indulgence for this book.

My books have been appreciated by thousands of readers who have contacted me via various platforms—

social media, emails, readers' reviews, blogs, etc., conveying how they connected with things I had to say. Keeping their feedback in mind, I am writing this one, my ninth, with the hope that it successfully helps the reader arrive at their own understanding of the vast knowledge in Indic scriptures and how this knowledge can be used in our daily lives.

—Ashutosh Garg

Part One

---

7 Chakras of Management

MULADHARA CHAKRA

Laying the Foundation, Creating Something New

The balanced and harmonious flow of energy through the seven chakras present in our body is considered essential for overall well-being. Similarly, business entities embody seven chakras that are essential for ensuring their growth, prosperity, progress and harmony.

The first among these is the Muladhara or the root chakra, considered the foundation of the chakra system. When balanced, it provides the foundation for personal growth and empowerment and helps us feel grounded in the present moment. In Hinduism, the concept of laying the foundation can be understood in four different ways.

The first is our actions and decisions in the present laying the groundwork for our future. Lord Krishna teaches Arjuna that the foundation for a successful and fulfilling life is to perform our duty without attachment to the outcome. This is also encapsulated in the law of *karma*, which states that every action has a consequence and that we will inevitably reap what we sow.

The second is the importance of cultivating positive

qualities within ourselves. This is contained in the concept of *sadhana*, which refers to the spiritual practice that we undertake for self-development.

The third will be the importance of family and community. Hinduism places great emphasis on the role of the family in shaping our lives. This is reflected in the concept of *dharma*, which refers to our duty or responsibility in life.

The fourth and last involves developing a sense of purpose and meaning in life. This has been captured via the concept of *swadharma*, which refers to our individual nature. The idea is that by aligning our actions with our true nature, we can find greater fulfilment in life.

Based on the above aspects, it can be concluded that success is not measured solely by material wealth or achievement, but by the degree to which an individual is able to fulfil their Dharma and contribute to the greater good. By laying a strong foundation and practising motivation, delegation and empowerment, individuals can achieve success both on a personal and broader societal sense.

MOTIVATION

तेजः क्षमा धृतिः शौचमद्रोहोनातिमानिता।
भवन्ति सम्पदं दैवीमभिजातस्य भारत।।

Cultivate vigour, patience, will and purity.
Avoid malice and pride.
Then you will achieve your destiny.

—*Bhagavad Gita, Chapter 16, Verse 3*

Of all the lessons on motivation that I can recall, the one that fascinated me the most was the story of Eklavya.

Eklavya, the son of a poor hunter, wanted to learn archery; so he approached Dronacharya and requested him to teach him archery. But Dronacharya, being the teacher of the Royal family, was not permitted to teach anyone else.

However, Eklavya was determined. He went home, made a statue of Dronacharya and started practising archery in front of his 'guru'. Through consistent practice, he became an outstanding archer. When Arjuna found out about Eklavya, he asked him who his teacher was and the response was 'Dronacharya'. Arjuna was upset and castigated his Guru for teaching Eklavya and making him better than Arjuna.

Upon hearing this, Dronacharya decided to meet Eklavya, knowing that he had never given him any lessons. On testing him, Dronacharya concluded that Eklavya's skills were unmatched, and he could become the best archer. When he asked Eklavya about his Guru, Eklavya showed him the statue.

In those days, it was a custom for a Guru to ask for Guru Dakshina. Dronacharya, in order to protect his student

Arjuna, asked Eklavya to give him his right thumb as Guru Dakshina. Without hesitation and knowing that he would never be able to shoot an arrow again, Eklavya cut off his right thumb as an offering and placed it at the feet of his Guru.

It was Eklavya's inner drive that made him the best archer without any formal training. Motivation is this inner drive that inspires us to perform specific actions or indulge in specific types of behaviour to achieve or gain something. These inner conditions, such as wishes, desires and goals, are activated, encouraging us to move in a particular direction and forming a behavioural pattern.

∞

According to various theories, motivation may be rooted in a basic need to minimize physical pain and maximize pleasure; or it may include specific needs such as eating and resting; or a desired object, goal, state of being and ideal; or it may be attributed to less-apparent reasons such as altruism, selfishness, morality or avoiding mortality.

Motivation thus gives us a sense of purpose. It keeps us focused and engaged, making life purposeful. It is often the driving force that pushes us to achieve our goals.

The motivation to do something can be both positive and negative. It could be drawn from anger, frustration, joy, care or any other emotion we feel as humans.

From the Vedic times, our seers probed and perceived human behaviour to understand the forces that drove people to do what they do and the reasons behind specific types of behaviour. They identified four major factors that motivated people:

- Dharma (righteousness or duty)

- Artha (wealth)
- Kama (sexual desire)
- Moksha (total freedom)

Our scriptures and seers understood motivation as a combination of our karma, desires and nature. Actions could be materialistic, spiritual, ethical or value-based. They believed that we must not only engage in selfish and profitable enterprises to benefit from the economics of prosperity and mass production but also free ourselves from any motivation to be selfish or self-centred. They believed that motivated actions were the cause of karma, suffering and rebirth.

Karma

We live our lives performing various types of acts and taking or not taking action. This is the law of life. Most of us act not because we want to take action but because we want the fruit of our actions. We thus need to understand our actions and forget their results, whether positive or negative.

We can escape from the bonds of karma only if we are able to renounce our desire for the results of our actions.

Desires

Our scriptures have a God for desire—Kama, the God of erotic love and pleasure. During the Vedic age, Kama personified cosmic desire or the creative impulse.

Most of us are driven by our desires. The Vedas affirm that we exist because of our desires. In seeking a quid pro quo for our actions, we keep our desires alive.

Desire arises from the continuous interaction of our

senses with worldly objects. Our desires can also be the result of our past lives.

It is believed that only Brahman is not motivated by desire and yet there are so many examples of our Gods and their desires in most of our scriptures.

GITA ON MOTIVATION

The *Gita* explains the Hindu theory of motivation as follows:

If you force someone to do some work, you get what you desire, but if you set him free and make him accountable or own that task, you will get more than you wanted.

The hopelessness and despair of Arjuna in the *Gita* are typical of a vulnerable human. Lord Krishna, through the sheer power of His inspiring words, changes Arjuna's mind from a state of inaction to one of righteous action and self-confidence.

Lord Krishna's sermon to Arjuna

1. *Lead by example:* 'Whatever the excellent and best ones do, the commoners follow', says Lord Krishna in the *Gita*. Thus, stick to the basics, set an example and try to lead by example. When the team sees the leader work hard, it motivates them to keep pace with the leader.
2. *Clarity of goals:* Each person has different perspectives and attitudes towards their work. What the *Gita* tells us is to have a larger vision in our work for a common purpose. Further, the purpose must have clarity so that people can focus on the attainment of goals. The leader thus needs to involve people in the communication process to create the goals to be achieved. If people are

involved in the process, they psychologically own the mission, vision, values and goals.

3. *Trust your team:* Lord Krishna had complete faith in Arjuna's ability, which in turn motivated him to fight in the battle against his family members. The leader needs to demonstrate that they believe in the abilities of their team members to live up to expectations, deliver their commitments and achieve their goals. This will also develop a sense of mutual accountability in the team.

4. *Stand by your team:* A leader must recognize and understand that most of us are afraid in uncertain times. Lord Krishna understood Arjuna's state of mind. We need to be available to our colleagues when they need us the most. As leaders, we need to be able to demonstrate that we are, like Lord Krishna, the *sarathi* (the driver of Arjuna's chariot) and are with the team, whatever the situation.

5. *When the going gets tough:* The *Gita* teaches us to be balanced during good times and bad times. The skill necessary in the performance of our duty is to maintain a balance in our mind when faced with success or failure. A calm mind in the face of failure will lead to deeper introspection, and we will be able to clearly see our mistakes so that corrective steps can be taken to avoid such shortcomings in the future.

THE SECRET SOURCE OF MOTIVATION

Our motivation differs for different types of actions. Some actions may be trivial while some may be life-changing. The variations occur because of our perception and motivation for each action or task.

We need to understand people and truly discern their motives and hidden agendas to understand what motivates them to do what they do. Thus, we need to understand the true source of motivation. If we constantly rationalize our actions and live in a state of self-denial, we will be unable understand the truth about ourselves.

Looking at ourselves in the mirror will help us unmask our own behaviour patterns.

My father often told me that when you look at yourself in the mirror and can tell yourself that you did not, knowingly, harm or hurt anyone the previous day, that is the only justification you would ever need in the world. Beyond this, nothing mattered. It is this self-realization that can help us understand our own motivations.

Our actions speak louder than our words.

Therefore, to truly understand the motivation of others, we need to understand the root cause of their behaviour and actions.

There is an interesting story on motivation in the *Ramayana* as well.

Lord Rama and his army knew that Sita was being held as a prisoner in Lanka. The question among the leaders that arose then was who among them would be able to jump across the ocean and take a message to Sita to tell her that Lord Rama was on his way to bring her back. The mighty ocean was big and rough, so the leaders started discussing how they would cross the ocean and also return.

Everyone was consulted regarding this issue. Whilst some did not have the ability to leap across the ocean, the ones who could were unsure if they would have the strength to return. Hanuman was listening to their discussions silently.

They turned to Hanuman and said 'Why are you silent? You surpass all of us in strength. You are equal to Rama and Lakshmana in terms of strength. You are like *Garuda*, the king of the birds; you can fly across the ocean. Your father, *Vayu*, the Wind God, promised your mother that you would be the mightiest and most intelligent. As a child, you flew towards the Sun to pluck it from the sky. By increasing your size, you will be able to cross the sea easily.'

This encouraged Hanuman and reminded him of his prowess. Hanuman agreed with great enthusiasm and faith to fly to Lanka. He then grew in size, crossed the ocean in a single leap and met Sita with the good news, returning safely.

This tells us that motivation is required from time to time to encourage and remind people of their potential.

It was something that even the mighty Hanuman needed.

∞

In a similar vein, as a manager, it is important to understand the relevance of motivation for the success and growth of an organization. Motivation refers to the inner drive that propels individuals to act and achieve their goals. In the context of management, motivation plays a crucial role in shaping the behaviour and performance of employees, which in turn impacts the overall performance of the organization.

Moreover, motivation also helps employees feel valued and appreciated for their contributions. A positive work environment, where employees feel motivated and valued, can lead to increased job satisfaction, lower turnover rates and reduced absenteeism. As a manager, it is important to understand the motivations and drives of your employees and use these to create a positive work environment.

∞

Yet another example will be from Chanakya's (375-283 BCE) teachings, as he had a deep understanding of human nature. He mentioned four *Upayas*—*Sama, Dama, Danda* and *Bheda*—as methods to achieve a solution in state politics to avoid conflicts (Arthashastra 2.10.47[*]). Similarly, in management, we can implement a system of motivation that includes these four in the following manner:

Sama or Consultation

This is the first step that should be taken whenever it appears that an employee is not working to their full potential. As their manager, you have to listen to them and gain clear insight into their side of the story. Senior managers can glean information from various sources, but the most advisable option is to get the full picture by directly listening to the concerned person. You can discuss and suggest various alternatives to solve any challenges that may have arisen. If the said problem needs external intervention, then outside experts can be called in for support.

Chanakya suggests that a wise man should not undertake any venture without consultation and should act only after reflection.' He also emphasizes the importance of seeking out different perspectives and considering all options before making a final decision.

---

[*]The numbers correspond to the chapter number, followed by the verse and serial numbers of the original text.

Dama or Reward

Employees work for wages and salaries, which are the key motivating factors for them to work for an organization. The next thing that they look for is honour. Without these two forms of encouragement, no employee will have any reason to continue working for an organization.

Chanakya suggests rewarding employees sufficiently to get work done. The reward could be in the form of incentives, paid perquisites, bonuses or promotions. Another way of rewarding employees is through recognition among their peers.

Danda or Punishment

Many employees may not show any signs of improvement despite constant prodding. In such cases, neither rewards nor incentives can bring them out of their lethargic state. This, then, becomes a serious situation and if not rectified, a sense of complacency can spread throughout the organization.

Chanakya recommends a stronger step for such erring employees, punishment. This can be subtle or cruel, depending on the person as well as the situation. It can take the form of a warning, a suspension, a cut in pay or a demotion.

Bheda or Severance

When the first three methods do not work, Chanakya recommends the fourth and the harshest step. When nothing is working, the only option left is to sever ties or part ways.

MANAGEMENT MANTRAS

Whether it's Eklavya's story, examples from the *Gita* and *Ramayana* or Chanakya's precepts, the common factor among them when related to management is that motivation drives employees to work hard and put in their best efforts. It helps them overcome obstacles and challenges and work sincerely towards their goals. When employees are motivated, they are more productive, creative and engaged in their work, contributing to the success of the organization. A motivated workforce is essential for organizations to remain competitive and achieve their goals.

As a manager, it is important to understand the relevance of motivation and use it to drive the performance and growth of the organization. To achieve this, managers can utilize various motivational tools and techniques such as providing recognition and rewards for good performance, offering opportunities for professional development and fostering an open and supportive work environment. Managers can also set clear goals and expectations and provide feedback and coaching to help employees reach their objectives.

In conclusion, motivation is a crucial factor in the success of an organization.

DELEGATION AND EMPOWERMENT

यद्यदाचरति श्रेष्ठस्तत्तदेवेतरो जन:।
स यत्प्रमाणं कुरुते लोकस्तदनुवर्तते।।

Whatever actions are performed by great men,
common men follow in their footsteps,
and whatever standards they set by exemplary acts,
all the world pursues.

—*Bhagavad Gita, Chapter 3, Verse 21*

In the *Mahabharata*, Lord Krishna empowered the Pandavas in every aspect; yet when it came to protecting Draupadi, He chose not to delegate the work to someone else but do it himself.

Similarly, Rishi Vyasa empowered Sanjaya with *divya drishti* to witness the Mahabharata war and narrate everything that is taking place to the blind King Dhritarashtra. Duryodhana, in contrast, delegated the responsibility of playing dice with Yudhishthira to Shakuni, knowing that Shakuni, with his skills, would ensure victory in the game of dice, achieving his aims.

Our scriptures are replete with amazing examples of delegation and empowerment, both of which are also useful management tools and techniques. Although both are used for the same purpose of employee management, they have some differences.

Delegation and empowerment are beneficial if used effectively; however, they are most effective when used specifically for a particular situation and are also dependent on the attitude of the manager and the organization. The key difference between the two techniques is that while empowerment raises leaders, delegation raises followers.

Let us have a look at what delegation and empowerment mean.

Delegation can be explained as the assignment of authority to another person to carry out specific and agreed-upon activities. It constitutes the process of distributing and entrusting work to another person, which is one of the core concepts of management leadership.

In contrast, empowerment means that the leader is confident in the abilities of their team. Empowerment, as a part of a company's culture, results in the creation of a more creative and efficient workforce. Research has also shown that employee engagement increases when individuals feel empowered.

In the *Ramayana* as well, there are quite a few instances where delegation and empowerment can be observed. One is Lord Rama helping Sugriva to win back his kingdom Kishkindha from Bali. In turn, Sugriva, with his army, helped Lord Rama. Another is when His army was unable to cross the mighty ocean, Lord Rama empowered Hanuman to cross it instead and deliver his message to Sita, who was imprisoned in Lanka by Ravana.

In these instances, Lord Rama understood the strengths and weaknesses of His team. That is the reason why Hanuman was assigned the task of finding Sita and reconfirming her presence in Lanka, based on his physical skill set and presence of mind.

Another instance is when Lord Rama sends Angada as His messenger to convince Ravana to peacefully return Sita. In the court of Ravana, as soon as Angada planted his foot on the ground, no one was able to move it. When Ravana himself tried to move Angada's foot, Angada moved it saying that Ravana should instead touch the feet of Lord Rama.

In this case, Angada was delegated a task of authority. He was a messenger deployed to discuss a peaceful resolution and avoid war. His skill set included assertiveness, authority and communication skills and he knew how and when to control his temper, which was not the case with Hanuman.

In all the above cases, Lord Rama observed and realized the strengths of his team members. He evaluated the situation and the member's skill set. He made sure of the circumstances and allowed his team to collaborate to get the desired results.

LESSONS ON DELEGATION AND EMPOWERMENT

According to the businesses they are running, leaders choose whether they want to delegate or empower. When a leader delegates, it means they give formal instructions to their employees and want them to act as they have been told with some creativity of their own. Conversely, when leaders empower, they give their employees full liberty to choose their path to do a specific job. Delegation and empowerment are thus compelling concepts when it comes to leading.

Delegation and empowerment are both essential for managers in today's fast-paced and complex business environment. They allow managers to get more done in less time and increase their efficiency and effectiveness in managing their teams and achieving their goals.

As far as delegation is concerned, the age-old norm that we can delegate authority but not responsibility holds true.

A leader can ask their subordinate to handle a task or project but if it does not go as planned, it is the leader who will ultimately be held responsible.

Apart from that, delegation results in improved relationships within the team. It helps avoid any conflict, as all the work is being delegated by someone senior to them. A healthy one-on-one relationship is built between the leader and the team as everyone reports individually. Delegation helps in improving time management, being more productive and increasing overall efficiency at work.

Chanakya's methods of delegation and empowerment

In ancient times, Chanakya developed the vision for his young ward Chandragupta Maurya and then motivated and empowered him to work towards realizing that vision. Once the task had been outlined and the process to achieve it had been defined, Chanakya ensured that all facilities were made available to the young Chandragupta Maurya to achieve the goals. This brings us to the steps that can be followed to either delegate work to or empower an individual.

Delegate work and empower an individual

1. Define the task
2. Select the individual or team
3. Outline a clear communication
4. State and explain the results expected from the task
5. Agree on the objectives and resources
6. Ensure that the task set is in line with the goals of the team and individual
7. Agree on the deadlines for the task

8. Support and communicate as the teams undertake the task
9. Provide regular feedback

Delegation refers to the process of assigning specific tasks or responsibilities to others within the organization, for example, to subordinates, peers or even superiors, depending on the nature of the task and the capability of the individuals involved. Delegation helps managers to offload some of their workloads and free up their time to focus on more important tasks that require their attention and expertise.

By delegating, managers can build a more skilled and competent workforce as employees are given opportunities to learn new skills, build their confidence and take on new responsibilities.

Empowerment, in contrast, refers to the process of giving employees the authority, resources and support they need to make decisions and take actions that contribute to the success of the organization. Empowerment enables employees to feel valued and engaged in their work, and it encourages them to take initiative and make meaningful contributions. By empowering employees, managers can create a positive work environment, increase motivation and productivity and foster a sense of ownership and accountability among their team members.

However, empowering could have its own costs as well. Some employees may abuse the authority they have been conferred with. Too much empowerment could also lead to misunderstandings between fellow workers.

MANAGEMENT MANTRAS

Both delegation and empowerment have relevance for managers in today's rapidly changing business environment. With the increasing demand for innovation and creativity, managers must be able to tap into the knowledge and skills of their employees to keep pace with the changing needs of their customers and the market.

By delegating tasks and empowering employees, managers can encourage a more diverse range of perspectives, generate new ideas and approaches and promote a culture of continuous improvement and learning. Further, managers can improve their efficiency and effectiveness, increase the skills and capabilities of their team members and foster a more positive work environment. With these concepts, managers can lead their organizations to greater success and meet the changing needs of their customers and the market.

Delegation and empowerment should be used as primary tools when leading your teams. They are powerful ways of diversifying the role of a team while keeping them motivated.

SUCCESS

यं यं लोकं मनसा संविभाति विशुद्धसत्त्व: कामयते यांश्च कामान्।
तं तं लोकं जयते तांश्च कामा स्तस्मादात्मज्ञं ह्यर्चयेद्भूतिकाम:॥

Those who understand the path of devotion and
the path of knowledge are considered fit for liberation.
Success is determined by the
aspirant's dedication and devotion.

—*Mundaka Upanishad,*[*] *Part 3, Section 1, Verse 10*

The typical themes in many scriptures of Hinduism are worldly life, acquiring wealth, professional competence, supernatural achievements, perfection in practice, excellence in moral and spiritual life, wars and conflicts between good and evil, victory and defeat, opulence, self-made men of great eminence, and the rise and fall of great heroes, cities, empires and kingdoms.

It may seem like a lot to take in, but Hinduism has never been averse to the idea of success or achievement. Rather, the Vedas recognize the right to enjoy as part of dharma and mortal existence. Enjoyment, not renunciation, is the very essence of life. In our prayers, we unhesitatingly seek the help of God to achieve name and fame, progeny, wealth, peace, happiness, strength, virility, courage, victory in war and success in attracting the love of our life.

However, there is a fine line between success and failure and a key factor is our determination. It often happens that

---

*The *Mundaka Upanishad* has three *Mundakams* (parts or shavings); each part has two *khanda* (section or volume), which further contain metered poetic verses. In total, the *Upanishad* features 64 mantras.

just when we are on the verge of succeeding, we succumb to temptation and leave the goal unaccomplished. The lack or presence of willpower determines whether we fail or accomplish our goals and achieve success.

If we look closely, success is a highly subjective concept that can mean different things to different people. For managers, success can be defined as the ability to achieve their goals and objectives in a timely and efficient manner. It can encompass a variety of aspects, including financial performance, employee morale, customer satisfaction and personal satisfaction. To be successful as a manager, one must have a clear understanding of what success means to them and work towards achieving it through careful planning, effective communication and strong leadership skills.

In Hindu scriptures, success is considered an important part of our lives. It is also referred to as *Artha*, which means an asset or something meaningful. In fact, Hinduism classifies success according to the stages of life: the first and second half of life.

In the first half, it is recommended that we pursue education, family, wealth and fame as essential to healthy and fulfilled living. Such success is necessary for security, continuity, predictability and control. We need to be strong and disciplined before we can let go of our egos.

We appreciate the success achieved in the first half of our life when we start the second half. The latter manifests itself as we go through what we can refer to as a mid-life crisis. This is when we start looking at new projects, relationships or careers while addressing the maximum commitments of our lives.

This is the juncture of our life when we start to find the true meaning of life: It's *Artha*. The question 'What is my essence? What is my calling? What is success?' can only be answered in the second half of our life if we have pursued the first half justly.

What the above tells us is that we can drive ourselves to be successful and realize later that we are becoming more distant from our true nature.

True success is not in achieving healthy and fulfilled living in the first half of life but in the unravelling of a deeper mystery of our authentic identity and relationship with this transient world.

Similarly, there is no guarantee that success will always make us happy, or failure will always be a painful experience. We can also draw from the lessons contained in our scriptures.

LESSONS ON SUCCESS FROM THE *GITA*

The *Gita* outlines the following guidelines for success.

1. *Our duty is our dharma*: Lord Krishna counsels Arjuna to fulfil his duty as a Kshatriya to establish the principles of dharma. He states that 'the main duty of a warrior is never to submit to anybody, and he must resist any impulse for self-preservation that would make him avoid a fight.'
2. *Everything happens for the good*: The *Gita* says 'Whatever happened, happened for good. Whatever is happening is happening for good. Whatever will happen will also happen for good.' We have heard this phrase from our elders and we pass on the same message to our children.

This simply means that behind every failure there is a bigger picture that we need to look at.

3. *Change is inevitable*: Everything is subject to the universal law of change. Material possessions and relationships will change. Nothing is permanent and the *Gita* asks us to embrace this change and start from scratch.
4. *Death is an opportunity to transcend*: The *Gita* states that for sure is the death of all that comes to birth, sure is the birth of all that dies. So, in a matter that no one can prevent, we have no cause to grieve. Death is not a calamity but a path to God.
5. *Hard times bring out the best in us*: Life will always be a challenge but difficult times will present lessons that we can learn from.
6. *Act without any expectations*: The main message of the *Gita* is to act without any expectations. We have the right to work but we do not have the right to expect a reward in return for our work.

In summary, the essence of success lies in the power of our belief.

MANAGEMENT MANTRAS

One of the key components of success for managers is setting clear and achievable goals. This requires careful consideration of the resources available, the needs of the employees and customers and the overall vision of the organization. A well-defined set of goals provides a roadmap for success and helps keep the team focused on what is important. It is important for managers to regularly evaluate their progress towards these goals and adjust their strategies as needed to ensure that they are on track to achieve success.

Another important aspect of success for managers is effective communication. Good communication skills are critical for creating a positive work environment and building strong relationships with employees and customers. Managers must be able to effectively convey their vision and goals and listen to the needs and concerns of others. They must also be able to provide constructive feedback and motivate and inspire their team to work together towards common goals.

Leadership is another essential ingredient in the recipe for success for managers. A good leader is able to inspire and guide their team to achieve their goals and foster a culture of collaboration and teamwork. Effective leadership skills include the ability to delegate responsibilities, make decisions and provide support and guidance to others. A good leader must also be able to build trust, establish credibility and effectively manage change and handle challenges as they arise.

Success for managers is a complex and multifaceted concept that encompasses a wide range of skills and abilities. It requires a clear understanding of what success means, careful goal setting, effective communication and strong leadership skills. By focusing on these key areas, managers can increase their chances of success and help their teams and organizations achieve their goals.

SVADHISTHANA CHAKRA

Invoking Shakti, Infusing Energy

The second is the Svadhisthana or the Sacral Chakra, linked to flexibility and adaptability. When balanced, it supports healthy and emotionally fulfilling connections with others as well as enhances artistic expression, innovation and the ability to think outside the box.

In Hinduism, *Shakti* is the divine feminine energy that represents the creative and transformative power of the universe. Invoking Shakti can bring happiness, help in handling tough adversaries and conquering fear.

By worshipping Shakti, one can tap into Her energy and experience a sense of inner happiness as She is the embodiment of joy and prosperity. Goddess Durga, who represents the invincible form of Shakti, is believed to grant material and spiritual prosperity, and her blessings are sought to achieve a life of contentment.

Durga is also known as *Mahishasuramardini*, the destroyer of the demon *Mahishasura*, who represents the ego, ignorance and negativity that we encounter in our lives. By invoking Shakti, we can overcome these negative energies and defeat our adversaries, whether within or on the outside.

Goddess Kali, who is said to have emerged from Durga, is also associated with overcoming adversity. She is often depicted holding a sword to cut through negativity and a severed head representing the ego that needs to be conquered.

Goddess Bhairavi, another fearsome form of Durga, represents the power of transformation. Her worship is believed to help us overcome fear and gain courage. Goddess Chamunda, identified with either Goddesses Durga or Kali and often depicted holding a trident, is also associated with the conquest of fear.

By invoking Goddesses Durga, Kali, Bhairavi and Chamunda, we can tap into the transformative power of Shakti and achieve happiness, handle tough adversaries and conquer fear by infusing our lives with Their energy, overcoming the challenges that life presents.

HAPPINESS

Happiness is achieved when what you think,
what you say and what you do are in harmony.

—*Mahatma Gandhi*

Buddha considered happiness as a fleeting part of *samsara*— the wheel of repeated birth, mundane existence and death. We usually try to cling to the state of happiness, whereas the wheel keeps turning, presenting us with both pleasure and pain in life.

But then, is happiness short-lived? Only when one tries to achieve it solely by possessing material things. Happiness is an emotional state characterized by feelings of joy, satisfaction, contentment and fulfilment. While we can feel happy because of any number of reasons, it is often described as involving positive emotions and satisfaction with one's life.

Furthermore, when most people discuss happiness, they either consider their feelings in that present moment or refer to a more general sense of how they feel about life. Yet happiness is not an end in itself.

In contrast, unhappiness is simply defined as the feeling of not being happy. We constantly go through the emotions of being happy or unhappy and may react accordingly to different situations that we face several times a day.

Thus, we experience unhappiness because of union and separation or attraction and aversion to the objects and conditions that we like or dislike. Another example will be our happiness when we are with those whom we like, or unhappiness when we are with those whom we dislike.

The other aspect of happiness, when we are able to observe happiness as a spectator, is probably because we are discovering it via a series of indulgences or distractions, which is also known as pleasure. Pleasure is often mistakenly referred to as happiness. We tend to label our greatest pleasure as our greatest happiness, whereas pleasure is only a form of gratification, stimulation or indulgence.

Indeed, one may experience temporary happiness in pursuing objects that impact our senses. However, it is a trap because the pursuit of objects results in attachment. From attachment arises karma, delusion and bondage, which aggravates our suffering and makes our chances of enjoying life increasingly difficult.

Osho says that happiness depends on where we are in our consciousness. Humanity can be classified into two types—the ones who are asleep and the ones who are awakened. If you are asleep, then pleasure is happiness. Pleasure then refers to the sensation that the body is being forced to achieve but is not usually capable of.*

Because happiness tends to be such a broadly-defined term, psychologists and other social scientists typically use the term 'subjective well-being' when they talk about this emotional state that focuses on an individual's overall personal feelings about their satisfaction with life.

HAPPINESS IN OUR SCRIPTURES

Our scriptures state that happiness in human life arises as a result of our own actions and past life karma as well as actions of Gods and others.

Lord Krishna says in the *Gita*, 'And now hear from me, O Arjuna, of the three kinds of happiness in which the embodied soul rejoices and can even reach the end of all suffering.'

1. *Satvik* or pure happiness: It is the happiness that arises from the elevation of the soul. However, attaining this isn't easy. One pursuing *satvik* or pure happiness has to

---

*'Osho on Happiness—Pleasure is Animal, Happiness is Human, Bliss is Divine', *Osho Teachings*, 25 August 2023, https://www.oshoteachings.com/osho-discourse-on-happiness-pleasure-is-animal-happiness-is-human-bliss-is-divine/.

practise a lot of discipline. That's why it feels like poison in the beginning but becomes nectar in the end.

This can also be defined as physical happiness, which arises from the comforts of life, sensual enjoyment and bodily pleasures.

2. *Rajasik* or result-oriented happiness: This is the materialistic pleasure that is derived when the senses come in contact with external objects that create a feeling of gratification. However, this kind of happiness is temporary.

This can also be understood as mental happiness, which arises from a sense of fulfilment and freedom from worries, afflictions and anxieties.

3. *Tamasic* or slothful happiness: This is the lowest form of happiness and is derived from sleeping or being lazy. The soul is never nurtured through these practices but because there is a tiny sense of pleasure associated with it, people wrongfully consider it to be a state of happiness.

This can also be understood as spiritual happiness, which arises from freedom from the cycle of births and deaths, and union with the Self.

The *Gita* contains 30 quotes on happiness, emphasizing various aspects of happiness that impact our lives.[*] One important quote that struck me as relevant in the present context is as follows:

---

[*]Sashi, '30 Bhagavad Gita Quotes on Happiness', *Vedicfeed*, 19 June 2023, https://vedicfeed.com/bhagavad-gita-quotes-on-happiness/.

कामक्रोधवियुक्तानां यतीनां यतचेतसाम्॥
अभितो ब्रह्मनिर्वाणं वर्तते विदितात्मनाम्॥

Those who are free from anger and all material desires,
who are self-realized, self-disciplined and
constantly endeavouring for perfection, are assured of
liberation now as well as in the near future.

—*Bhagavad Gita, Chapter 5, Verse 26*

The idea of achieving true happiness through a peaceful state of mind and union with God is a cornerstone of many spiritual traditions, including the paths described in the *Bhagavad Gita*.

Did you know that happiness has been viewed through different lenses by scriptures from around the world?

It is believed that good karma sets us on the path of achieving happiness. In contrast, the impediments to achieving peace and happiness are as follows:

1. Ego (*aham*)
2. Ignorance (*avidya*)
3. Impurities (*malas*)
4. Delusion (*maya*)
5. Past actions (*karma*)
6. Desire (*kama*) and
7. Attachments (*pasas*)

Hindu scriptures consider both material and spiritual needs that could impact happiness. Our scriptures recognize four areas that lead to happiness: religious and moral duty (*dharma*), wealth (*artha*), conjugal bliss (*kama*) and liberation (*moksha*), which can further be explained as follows:

1. Religious and moral duty (dharma): By pursuing *dharma*, we can enjoy name, fame and respect in the society we live in.
2. Wealth (artha): With *artha* comes the enjoyment of the physical comforts of life, status in society and the satisfaction that we will be in a position to fulfil our commitment to our family and society.
3. Conjugal bliss (kama): *Kama* ensures our happiness through conjugal bliss, companionship with our spouse and love for our children and family.
4. Liberation (moksha): *Moksha*, the ultimate goal of all Hindus, enables us to pursue liberation so that we can achieve eternal happiness and complete freedom from all our worldly obligations.

Our happiness is also linked to the four phases of human life as defined in our scriptures. These are *Brahmacharya, Grihastha, Vanaprastha* and *Sanyasa*:

1. *Brahmacharya* corresponds to childhood and youth. This is the period when we complete our education and learn about our duties and responsibilities (dharma) as responsible members of our society. In addition, we also learn about ourselves and the supreme self.
2. *Grihastha* corresponds to adult life. During this phase, we perform our duties (dharma) and earn wealth (artha), thereby working towards fulfilling our responsibilities to our family and society.
3. *Vanaprastha* corresponds to old age. During this phase,

as senior citizens, we work towards understanding our journey in fulfilling our dharma, contemplate the wisdom we would have gained through our journey in life and seek to understand the ultimate purpose of human life, leading to moksha or liberation.
4. *Sanyasa* is the last phase of human life. This is the phase when we renounce everything and work for moksha.

Life's journey generally goes through these phases. As we get older, our desire to understand our own life and its relationship with dharma, karma and moksha becomes far more important and pronounced.

THE TEN STEPS TO HAPPINESS

Mahatma Gandhi outlined the following 10 steps to happiness[*]:

1. When I despair, I remember that all through history the way of truth and love have always won.
2. A man is but the product of his thoughts. What he thinks, he becomes.
3. Seek not greater wealth, but simpler pleasure; not higher fortune, but deeper felicity.
4. Satisfaction lies in the effort, not in the attainment. Full effort is full victory.
5. An eye for an eye will only make the whole world blind.

---

[*] '10 Quotes by Mahatma Gandhi on Life & Happiness', *Mamiverse*, https://mamiverse.com/mahatma-ghandi-quotes-life-happiness-50307/ and 'Gandhi's Ten Steps to Happiness', *Globalization ICAS*, https://globalizationicas.com/creative-lounge/gandhis-ten-steps-to-happiness/.

6. Be the change you want to see in the world.
7. The straight path is as difficult as it is simple; were it not so, all would follow the straight path.
8. Each one has to find his peace from within. And peace to be real must be unaffected by outside circumstances.
9. The best way to find yourself is to lose yourself in the service of others.
10. Live as if you were to die tomorrow. Learn as if you were to live forever.

Achieving happiness is a complex endeavour, as it involves a combination of internal and external factors, and what works for one person might not necessarily work for another.

Following are 10 steps towards achieving a state of happiness:

1. Self-awareness: Begin by understanding yourself. Recognize your feelings, thoughts and triggers. Journaling, mindfulness and meditation can help improve self-awareness.
2. Gratitude: Cultivate a sense of gratitude. Start a gratitude journal and note down three things you're grateful for every day. This can shift your focus from what is lacking in your life to what you already have.
3. Healthy lifestyle choices: Physical health plays a vital role in mental well-being. Regular exercise, a balanced diet and adequate sleep can significantly improve mood and reduce feelings of anxiety and depression.
4. Build strong relationships: Social connections are crucial for happiness. Foster meaningful relationships with family and friends. Make time for social activities and engage in open communication.

5. Pursue passion and purpose: Find activities that bring you joy and align with your personal values. Set goals and strive for growth, whether personal or professional.
6. Mindfulness and meditation: Engage in practices that keep you present, such as mindfulness and meditation. They can help reduce stress, improve focus and enhance overall well-being.
7. Limit negative inputs: Reduce exposure to negative news or toxic relationships. Set boundaries and curate your environment to support your well-being.
8. Continuous learning: Embrace new experiences and opportunities to learn. Whether it is picking up a new hobby, reading a book or taking a course, continuous learning stimulates the mind and brings satisfaction.
9. Resilience and coping skills: Life is full of challenges. Developing resilience helps you bounce back from setbacks. This could involve reframing negative thoughts, seeking support when needed and focusing on solutions rather than problems.
10. Seek professional help: If feelings of unhappiness persist or if you are struggling with issues like depression or anxiety, seek help from a therapist or counsellor. They can provide tools, strategies and support to navigate complex emotions.

KEY COMPONENTS OF HAPPINESS

Happiness is something we all crave, but while seeking happiness we forget that we ourselves can become obstacles. The desire for innumerable materialistic desires often leads to grief and dissatisfaction. Once we achieve one desire there is an urge for another. This vicious circle of desire is never-ending.

Our scriptures clearly and emphatically recognize that suffering is inherent to earthly life and trace its root cause to desire. We are unhappy because we are bound to impermanent things and cannot easily escape from their attraction and aversion to ourselves.

Because we are driven by our desire for impermanent things, our happiness on earth remains temporary and elusive. No one is free from suffering because of impermanence. This manifests itself in our lives as losses, ageing, sickness, decay, death and destruction.

Thus, we can conclude that the two key components of happiness are:

- *Balance of emotions:* Everyone experiences both positive and negative emotions, feelings and moods. Happiness is generally linked to experiencing more positive feelings.
- *Satisfaction in life:* This relates to how satisfied you feel with different areas of your life, including your relationships, work, achievements and other things that you consider important.

MANAGEMENT MANTRAS

As a manager, one is tasked with overseeing the operations of a company, ensuring that everything runs smoothly and efficiently. However, this often comes at a cost, as the demands of the role can become overwhelming and stressful. In this context, it is easy to overlook the significance of happiness for managers. However, the truth is that happiness is critical for the success of managers and consequently, the organizations they lead.

Research indicates that happiness has a significant impact on one's performance and productivity. Happy individuals tend to be motivated and engaged in their work, which leads to higher levels of performance. Moreover, happy individuals have a positive outlook, which can translate to increased creativity and problem-solving skills. This, in turn, can lead to effective decision-making, which is crucial for managers. As such, managers need to cultivate a happy and positive work environment, which can improve not only their performance but also of the other employees.

Happiness is also essential for building strong relationships within the workplace. Happy individuals tend to be approachable and easy to work with, which can foster better relationships with colleagues. In a manager's role it is important to maintain positive relationships with employees as this can increase morale and motivation.

In addition, happiness has a significant impact on one's overall well-being. Managers are often under immense pressure to meet deadlines, handle multiple tasks and manage employees, which can lead to stress and burnout. Happy individuals tend to be resilient and are able to handle stress better. This can reduce the risk of burnout and ensure that managers are able to maintain a healthy work–life balance.

Thus, happiness can improve a manager's overall well-being, reducing the risk of stress and burnout. It is critical for managers to prioritize their happiness and well-being, and to create a positive work environment that fosters the same among employees. By doing so, managers can ensure that they are able to perform at their best and help their organizations to succeed.

HANDLING A TOUGH ADVERSARY

कुतस्त्वा कश्मलमिदं विषमे समुपस्थितम्।
अनार्यजुष्टमस्वर्ग्यमकीर्तिकरमर्जुन।।
क्लैब्यं मा स्म गमः पार्थ नैतत्त्वय्युपपद्यते।
क्षुद्रं हृदयदौर्बल्यं त्यक्त्वोत्तिष्ठ परन्तप।।

It is not wise for an intelligent being
to lament at a time of crisis.
You should not be weak at the time of adversity;
you should fight adversities with a brave heart.

—*Bhagavad Gita, Chapter 2, Verses 2-3*

After a long journey to rescue Sita from Ravana's captivity in Lanka, Rama and Lakshmana camped on the outskirts of Ravana's kingdom along with their army.

War was imminent.

As the youngest brother of Ravana, Vibhishana was a relatively minor character in *Ramayana*. Yet his role became very important when he confronted his older brother Ravana on the grounds of dharma. He described the abduction of Sita as an act of *adharma* and advised Ravana to free her. When Ravana rejected his advice and asked him to leave, Vibhishana crossed over to Rama's side. He revealed several secrets of Ravana and his kingdom that proved to be game changers in the ensuing battle.

Interestingly, Kumbhakarna, the other brother of Ravana, too, flagged the immorality of Sita's abduction, but he stayed with his brother, the King, to fight against Rama and Lakshmana.

In the final battle between Rama and Ravana, when Rama was unable to kill Ravana, Vibhishana revealed the secret of Ravana's death to Rama. He told Rama that Ravana had the nectar of immortality stored in his belly. Unless this nectar was destroyed, Ravana could not be defeated. Rama fired his arrow at the *nabhi* (the belly button) of Ravana and that led to the fall of Ravana.

We too are often faced with challenges in our lives and careers that, at that moment, seem insurmountable. These challenges could be with respect to our colleagues, competitors, bosses or in other situations.

Most of us go through the fight-or-flight reaction: We either choose to stay and fight or we choose to run away. When we choose to fight, it is generally without any thought or strategy. We react to the situation and respond either with raised voices or physically if we believe we have the strength to overcome our opponent.

When faced with a tough adversary or a seemingly impossible situation, we need to look for our adversary's weak spot. We need to identify that one vulnerability that will disarm our opponent.

THE STORY OF DRONACHARYA

Dronacharya was becoming impossible to defeat. He was a master of the weapons of war and had several divine weapons with him, including the entire armoury of

Parashurama. After he was appointed the Commander-in-Chief of the Kaurava Army subsequent to the fall of Bhishma on the 10th day, he vowed to capture Yudhishthira and end the war. He failed four times.

On the 13th day, Drona configured the *Chakravyuha* where Abhimanyu was killed, following which Arjuna took a vow to avenge his son's death and kill Jayadratha. On the 14th day, there was a fierce battle between Drona and Arjuna, and later, Arjuna managed to get away from Drona and was able to kill Jayadratha with the help of Krishna.

On the night of the 14th day after the death of Jayadratha, Krishna told the Pandava camp that they needed to strategize to remove Dronacharya from the battlefield. Krishna reminded them that Dronacharya's son Ashwatthama was his biggest weakness.

Knowing it would be impossible to defeat Dronacharya in a fair battle, Krishna suggested to the Pandavas a plan to disarm their teacher. He suggested that Bhima kill an old elephant on the battlefield named Ashwatthama. Bhima did this and loudly proclaimed that he had killed Ashwatthama. This shook Dronacharya but he decided to get a confirmation from Yudhishthira as he knew that Yudhishthira would not speak an untruth. Several versions of Yudhishthira's response are available. Some say that he said 'Ashwatthama is dead, the elephant and not your son'. Under instructions from Krishna, the Pandava warriors blew their conches so loudly that Dronacharya only heard the first part of the statement. Others say that Yudhishthira spoke very softly so that Dronacharya heard only the first part. What is generally believed is that after this lie, Yudhishthira's flying chariot fell down to earth.

Dronacharya was unable to accept the death of his son and laid down his arms. He disembarked from his chariot and sat down in meditation. The Pandavas wanted to use this opportunity to arrest Dronacharya but enraged by the death of his father and several Panchala warriors, Dhrishtadyumna took this opportunity and beheaded Dronacharya in a gross violation of the rules of war. This angered the Pandavas but Krishna calmed them down, justifying the beheading as a consequence of Dronacharya's role in Abhimanyu's death.

Several moral discussions have taken place regarding these stories and much has been written about them. While these discussions will continue, I will refrain from getting into the morality aspect.

What is interesting to note and understand is that Dronacharya is usually questioned for his *adharma*, while Vibhishana is questioned for his *dharma*:

1. Should Dronacharya have taken the side of the Kauravas and gone against the Pandavas?
2. Should *Dharmaraj* Yudhishthira have lied to win a war?
3. Should Vibhishana have betrayed his brother, his king and his country and crossed over to the side of what he believed to be *dharma* and righteousness?

The lesson contained in both these stories is the importance of planning and thinking through the situation we are faced with rather than reacting immediately. We need to consider the situation from all angles. Dharma and adharma need to be interpreted as per the context of the situation instead of a purist interpretation of the matter under consideration.

As a young manager, I learnt that I must not react immediately when confronted with a challenge. I learnt that every challenge needs to be carefully thought through before committing myself to a response.

I learnt that I must never reply to any e-mail in anger. Even today if I am confronted with a challenging situation and thinking of sending an angry response, I compose the message at night and leave it in my outbox and 'sleep over it'. As it happens, there has not been one instance where I have not changed my response after sleeping over the problem!

MANAGEMENT MANTRAS

As a manager, one of the greatest challenges you may face is managing a tough adversary. This could be a difficult co-worker, a challenging customer or even a demanding boss. Regardless of the source of the conflict, it's important to approach the situation with a level head and a clear plan of action.

The first step in managing a tough adversary is to understand the root cause of the conflict. Is the individual difficult because they are trying to protect their own interests? Or are they simply hard to work with due to their personality or style? Understanding the cause of the conflict will help you determine the best course of action.

Once you have a clear understanding of the situation, the second step will be to approach the adversary with a positive and constructive attitude. This means being assertive but not aggressive and seeking to find a mutually acceptable solution. Try to avoid personal attacks and instead focus on the issue at hand.

One effective strategy for managing a tough adversary is active listening. Pay attention to what the other person is saying and try to understand their perspective. Show them that you value their input and are open to finding a solution that works for both of you. This can build trust and reduce the level of tension in the situation.

Another strategy for managing a tough adversary is to set clear boundaries and expectations.

Let the individual know what you expect from them in terms of behaviour and performance. Be firm but fair, and make sure to follow through with consequences if the boundaries are not respected. This can reduce the likelihood of future conflicts.

It is also important to practise effective communication skills when dealing with a tough adversary. This means avoiding sarcasm, being clear and concise and avoiding defensiveness. When communicating with the adversary, try to stick to the facts and avoid getting emotional. This will help to keep the situation from escalating and make it easier to find a resolution.

It is vital to recognize that not all conflicts can be resolved. In some cases, the best course of action may simply be to manage the situation and avoid confrontation. In these cases, it may be helpful to seek the support of a mediator or a human resources representative.

Finally, it is important to recognize that managing a tough adversary is an ongoing process. It requires patience, persistence and a commitment to finding a resolution. It may take time, but by approaching the situation with a positive attitude and effective communication skills, you can effectively manage a tough adversary and maintain a productive and positive work environment.

Managing a tough adversary can be a challenging experience, but it is possible to overcome with the right approach.

By understanding the root cause of the conflict, approaching the situation with a positive attitude, setting clear boundaries, practising effective communication skills and seeking support when necessary, we can effectively manage a tough adversary and maintain a productive and positive work environment.

CONQUERING FEAR

As soon as fear approaches, confront and destroy it.

—Chanakya

Lord Krishna says that 'every time we experience fear we must remember that at the same time, there is something fearless inside us too. Every time we doubt ourselves there is a part of us that is confident. Every time we are sad there is a part of us that is still happy. Write these down and fear will never overtake you. Whenever you feel fear read into it and know you can be fearless.'

Fear is a simple four-letter word that can have a significant impact on our lives. We would not be human if we said we do not have any fears. However, it is important to overcome our fears and manage the emotions that accompany our fears. We must accept and tame our fears.

Fear is possibly the single most important factor responsible for the development of our civilization. Our fear of the unknown, of the perils of nature, of the insecurities of forest life and of being alone and vulnerable led to the emergence of communities and civilized life and all the good things that came out of them, including the orderly society in which we live today with a certain degree of freedom, dignity and feelings of security.

Fear is a natural, emotional and instinctive response to a perceived threat. Fear is our single most experienced emotion and is the most dominant undercurrent in our consciousness. Most of our thoughts and actions are induced by our fears. In fact, we spend our whole lives trying to cope with our fears and find effective remedies or defences against them. Depending upon how we react to them, our fears may act either as destabilizing or motivating factors in our lives.

Fear can manifest in various ways, both physically and psychologically. Different individuals might experience fear differently, depending on their past experiences, personal resilience and current circumstances.

Here are some common ways in which fear can manifest itself:

Physical symptoms

1. Fight-or-flight response: Rapid heartbeat, quickened breathing, muscle tension, dilated pupils and heightened senses.
2. Stomach disturbances: Nausea, stomach cramps or a 'butterflies in the stomach' sensation.
3. Trembling or shaking: Especially in the hands or legs.
4. Sweating: Particularly in the palms, feet or forehead.

Behavioural symptoms

1. Avoidance: Evading situations, places or people associated with the fear.
2. Hyper-vigilance: Being extremely alert or watchful, even in non-threatening situations.

Psychological symptoms

1. Anxious thoughts: Obsessing over potential threats or negative outcomes.
2. Difficulty in concentrating: Being preoccupied with the source of fear.
3. Irritability: Becoming easily agitated or upset.

Emotional symptoms

1. Mood swings: Rapid changes in emotional state, often without a clear reason.
2. Feelings of guilt or shame: Especially if one believes their fear is irrational or that they shouldn't be afraid.

It is worth noting that everyone experiences fear in their own way. If fear begins to interfere with daily life or becomes persistent, it's a good idea to seek guidance from a professional.

All of us have our own ways of coping with our fears.

My mother taught me to recite the 40 verses of the *Hanuman Chalisa* when I was confronted with fear, which I have done since I was a child. I also chant the Gayatri Mantra when I am confronted with uncertainty or a challenge. Repeated recitation helps the mind understand the deeper meanings and nuances of what we continually say.

Our scriptures have mentioned fears and their debilitating effects. We can manage most of our fears by becoming aware of them through self-introspection. By being mindful and alert we can face our fears and understand them.

भूमिरापोऽनलो वायुः खं मनो बुद्धिरेव च।
अहङ्कार इतीयं मे भिन्ना प्रकृतिरष्टधा॥

—*Bhagavad Gita, Chapter 7, Verse 4*

Lord Krishna says in the *Bhagavad Gita*, 'now I shall reveal to you the greatest knowledge. The earth, water, fire, air, space, mind, intellect and ego are the eightfold components of our nature. Know that all beings are born with dual nature; our lower nature consists of emotions such as fear, but we also have a higher nature. So even when you are experiencing fear your consciousness is always fearless. You just need to tap into it.'

Fear, an inherent human emotion, has played a pivotal role in our evolutionary journey. It has been our alarm system, alerting us to threats and ensuring our survival. Yet, while the primordial fears of our ancestors focused on immediate physical threats, today's fears often stem from psychological, societal or imagined sources. This shift has profound effects on our minds and bodies, and the question beckons: can the human mind ever be truly devoid of fear?

At its core, fear is a protective mechanism. When confronted with a threat—the amygdala—the brain's centre for emotions, triggers a cascade of responses. These can include heightened senses, rapid heartbeat and a rush of adrenaline. In the short term, these physiological changes can be life-saving. However, when fear is chronic or misdirected, it can be debilitating. Persistent fear can lead to anxiety disorders, phobias and a host of other mental health issues. The stress hormones released during prolonged periods of fear can also impair cognitive function, memory and decision-making. Moreover, fear can isolate us, as we avoid situations or people we associate with potential harm.

Socially, fear is a double-edged sword. It can unite communities against a common threat, but it can also divide. Fear of the 'other', whether it be a different culture, race or belief system, can be manipulated to justify prejudice, discrimination or even violence. The ripple effects of such fears can resonate for generations, perpetuating cycles of mistrust and misunderstanding.

However, the aspiration to rid our mind of fear is an age-old quest, present in philosophical traditions, religious teachings and modern psychotherapy. Many argue that while we may not eliminate fear entirely, we can learn to understand and manage it. Through practices like mindfulness, meditation and cognitive behavioural therapy, individuals can recognize their fears, discern their roots and respond rather than react.

In conclusion, while fear is deeply embedded in our psyche, the human spirit continuously seeks ways to transcend it. A mind entirely devoid of fear may remain an idealistic notion but with awareness and effort, we can certainly mitigate its harmful effects and embrace a life of courage and clarity.

From a spiritual perspective, fear is an indication of ego and lack of trust in oneself and God. If we believe we are all alone and have to face the hurdles of life ourselves, we are faced with anxiety, fear and uncertainty.

Most of our fears could be either irrational or imaginary.

We can learn to deal with them firmly and realistically, with awareness, attention, maturity and understanding. We must never surrender to our fears. This may give us temporary relief but will not help us overcome our fears.

In Tibetan Buddhism, monks use a special visualization technique to gain control over their fears. This practice is said to have been introduced in Tibet. In this practice, monks spend time in a place usually avoided by ordinary people such as a graveyard, a dark cave or an underground cellar in the dark or the middle of the night all by themselves to practise meditation. During this, they visualize their fears, giving shape to them in detail and feeding them mentally, with compassion, to ferocious monsters and hungry demons. The technique is said to be very effective in exorcising one's fears permanently and bringing peace and quiet to one's mind.

∞

In *Chanakya Niti*, Chanakya says, 'A hard-working person cannot remain poor, a person who continuously remembers God is unlikely to perform a sin, a person with peace cannot quarrel. Similarly, a vigilant person has no fears.'

Fear, often perceived negatively, also has a positive aspect; it is intended by nature as a protective mechanism to safeguard us against the perils of life.

Following are some positive aspects of fear:

1. Survival and evolutionary role: Historically, fear played a vital role in the survival of our ancestors. It alerted them to potential dangers like predators or harmful situations, enabling them to either face the threat (fight) or escape it (flight).

2. Motivation: Fear can motivate individuals to prepare or take action. For example, the fear of failing an exam might motivate a student to study harder.
3. Preparedness: Fear of potential future threats can lead individuals or communities to prepare in advance, such as taking precautions for natural disasters or saving money for potential future economic downturns.
4. Enhanced awareness: Fear heightens our senses and awareness of our surroundings, making us more attuned to details that we might overlook in a relaxed state.
5. Setting boundaries: Fear helps us set boundaries to protect our physical and emotional well-being. For example, if someone has a fear of heights, they might avoid precarious ledges, reducing the risk of accidental falls.
6. Personal growth: Facing our fears can be a source of personal growth. Overcoming challenges and confronting what we are afraid of can boost self-confidence and resilience.
7. Moral compass: Sometimes, fear serves as a reminder of the potential consequences of our actions, encouraging ethical and moral behaviour. The fear of repercussions or societal judgment can steer people away from making harmful decisions.
8. Physiological responses: Fear releases adrenaline, preparing the body to respond to threats. This boost can improve performance in some situations, like sports or emergencies, where quick reflexes and heightened awareness are beneficial.
9. Encourages caution: Fear can make us more cautious, prompting us to think twice before making decisions, especially when potential risks are involved.

10. Stimulates change: Fear of stagnation or being left behind can drive innovation and the pursuit of new knowledge or skills.

While chronic or excessive fear can be debilitating and counterproductive, moderate and situation-appropriate fear has shaped human evolution and can serve as a tool for self-improvement and protection.

We find a reflection of our own fears and aspirations as well as of what we are and what we think. Our fears are born out of our belief that we are separate from the Creator. We are afraid because we do not believe that God is with us.

MANAGEMENT MANTRAS

Fear is a powerful emotion that can profoundly impact our thoughts, feelings and actions. It can hold us back from reaching our full potential and achieving our goals, particularly in the workplace.

Fear can manifest itself in various forms, including the fear of failure, fear of public speaking, fear of change and fear of the unknown. These fears can limit our ability to take risks, make decisions and embrace new challenges. As a result, we may miss out on opportunities for growth, advancement and innovation.

One of the primary ways to conquer fear is to understand and acknowledge it. It is important to recognize when fear is holding you back and identify the specific triggers that cause it. This can help in gaining a better understanding of yourself and your emotional state and develop strategies to overcome your fears.

Another effective way to conquer fear is to take action. This could mean speaking up in a meeting, volunteering for a challenging project or trying a new activity that you've been avoiding. By facing your fears head-on, you will become more confident and resilient. Additionally, taking small steps towards your goal can build momentum and help you feel more in control.

Challenging negative thought patterns is another key aspect of overcoming fear. Our thoughts and beliefs play a significant role in shaping our emotional state, and it's easy to get caught up in negative self-talk. To combat this, try to reframe your thoughts and focus on the positive aspects of a situation. This can help you build a more positive outlook and reduce feelings of anxiety.

For managers, overcoming fear is particularly vital, not only for their personal growth and development but also for the success and effectiveness of their team and the organization as a whole.

If a manager is afraid of public speaking, for example, they may be less likely to communicate effectively with their team and stakeholders. If a manager is afraid of failure, they may be less likely to take risks and innovate.

By conquering their fears, managers can become more confident and assertive leaders who are open-minded and flexible and are better equipped to make decisions, respond to new challenges and opportunities, manage conflict and motivate their teams. Additionally, by demonstrating resilience and a growth mindset, they can create a positive and supportive work environment where their team members feel encouraged to take risks, embrace new challenges and grow.

Moreover, overcoming fear can help managers develop a more flexible and adaptive leadership style. In today's fast-paced and rapidly changing business environment, it's essential for managers to be able to adapt to new circumstances and embrace change.

Conquering fear is an important aspect of personal and professional growth, particularly for managers. By understanding, acknowledging and taking action to overcome their fears, managers can become more confident, effective and adaptive leaders. This, in turn, can have a positive impact on the success and performance of their team and the organization as a whole.

MANIPURA CHAKRA

Courage and Mental Resolve

The third is the *Manipura* or the Solar Plexus Chakra, associated with personal power, confidence and self-esteem. When balanced, it helps individuals set and pursue goals with focus and resilience. Courage and mental resolve are two essential traits for an individual to thrive in today's world. The ability to withstand difficult situations and overcome obstacles with a determined and positive attitude is what sets successful individuals apart from the rest. However, it is not always easy to maintain such a state of mind, especially when faced with negative influences that can weigh us down.

Negative influences, whether internal or external, can be detrimental to our mental well-being and sap our courage and resolve. These could be negative thoughts, self-doubt, criticism from others or unfavourable circumstances that can impact our confidence and motivation. Another significant factor that can negatively affect our mental resolve is anger. Anger is a natural emotion, but if not managed properly, it can lead to negative outcomes.

Lord Hanuman is an excellent example of how to manage

anger effectively. Hanuman was known for his immense strength and courage, but he was also known for his calm and composed demeanour.

The lesson we can learn from Hanuman's character is that it is possible to channel our anger into a positive force rather than letting it control us.

NEGATIVE INFLUENCES ON OUR MIND

विज्ञानसारथिर्यस्तु मन:प्रग्रहवान्नर:।
सोऽध्वन: पारमाप्नोति तद्विष्णो: परमं पदम्।।

'As a strong wind sweeps away a boat on the water,
even one of the wandering senses on which the mind focuses
can carry away a man's intelligence.'

—*Katha Upanishad, Chapter 1, Section 3, Verse 9*

Emperor Akbar had a barber who was always very happy, even within his limited means. The emperor would often wonder why the barber was always happy whereas he, Akbar, who had everything he could have hoped for, was always stressed and unhappy.

Therefore, Akbar asked his trusted advisor Birbal the reason for the barber's happiness. Birbal was a wise person and told the emperor to put the poor barber in the 'circle of 99'. At night, Birbal put 99 gold coins in a bag and threw it inside the barber's house. The next morning, when the barber came to see Akbar, he was worried and tired.

The barber, who was used to living happily within his limited means, was now under self-imposed pressure to obtain one more gold coin to make it 100 coins.

The learning from this Akbar–Birbal folk tale is that we should not allow our mind to constantly dwell on material possessions; otherwise, we will lose our peace of mind.

∞

There are six temptations or sins that are universally accepted across all religions: Greed (or *lobha*), Lust *(kama)*, Anger *(krodha)*, Delusion or Ego *(moha)*, Pride *(mada)* and Jealousy *(matsarya or irshya)*. These can be considered the six enemies of the mind.

My interpretations of these temptations or sins will be from the perspective of how these negative influences can impact our minds and, as a result, our work.

Ramakrishna Paramahansa illustrated how a man's greed led to misery through his parable of a barber and the seven jars of greed.

A man was walking along a forest when a *yaksha* (spirits with magical powers) asked him if he wanted seven jars full of gold coins. The man told the yaksha that he would be glad to be the recipient of such an unexpected boon. The yaksha instructed him to go home, assuring that seven pots of gold would be waiting for him. The man hurried home. There, as the yaksha had promised, were seven pots of gold. But there was just one small problem: six of the jars were full while the seventh jar was only half full.

The man could have been content with the six full jars and the half-full jar. But such is the nature of greed that the man wanted to fill up the half-empty jar. So he sold whatever he owned to fill the jar. He almost lost his mental balance as he lost all his possessions but could still not fill the seventh jar. The King, on hearing his predicament, said to him, 'The yaksha made the same offer to me. I asked the yaksha, "When you talk about seven jars of gold, do you mean I can spend that wealth or is it merely for hoarding?" What seems like a sudden benefit usually comes with riders. Thus, we should not be greedy.'

∞

When I founded Guardian Pharmacy in India, I used to spend a lot of time with the new hires. Given all the temptations that existed in a store full of merchandise, which could either be consumed or pilfered, I would tell every new colleague three things that every parent also tells their child:

1. Do not steal
2. Do not lie
3. Fear God

Yet we had innumerable instances of stocks being pilfered and sold for cash. I often wondered what could have driven young individuals, who must have grown up with a strong set of values, to steal. Was it greed to get rich quickly or was it peer pressure to acquire more within this lifetime? Because of what we see around us, our mind keeps telling us to aspire for more and more.

We already know in our hearts and minds that lust, anger, greed, delusion, pride and jealousy are wrong. We need to be aware of these temptations and control ourselves. We also need to introspect to understand what makes us slip towards any of these temptations.

त्रिविधं नरकस्येदं द्वारं नाशनमात्मनः।
कामः क्रोधस्तथा लोभस्तस्मादेतत्त्रयं त्यजेत्।।

—*Bhagavad Gita, Chapter 16, Verse 21*

In the above verse, Lord Krishna says, 'There exist three gates that lead our souls to the hell of self-destruction—lust, anger and greed. Thus, we should strive towards abandoning all three.'

Lust, anger and greed are the foundations from which vices develop. They foster within the mind and make it a suitable ground for all other vices to take root. Krishna labels them as gateways to hell and strongly advises to shun them to avoid self-destruction.

∞

'The Goose that Laid the Golden Eggs' is one of Aesop's fables, which again narrates the pitfalls of excessive greed. There was a goose that would give its owner one golden egg every morning. One day, the owner became greedy and decided that he needed to take out all the eggs 'inside' the goose. He cut open the goose, killing it, and the answer was clear. The short-sighted action of killing the goose (that greed made him do) destroyed the long-term profitability of the asset (the goose that laid golden eggs every day).

Buddhism also contains several lessons on greed.

The three poisons for human beings are greed (*raga*), anger or hate (*dvesha*) and ignorance or delusion (*moha*). It is interesting to note that these vices or sources of evil are known as poisons in Buddhism.

Greed simply means wanting a little bit more or not being satisfied with what we have. We want more money, a bigger house, a better car or a promotion at work. All of us have so many wants.

Normally, we would never think of ourselves as greedy. Buddhism teaches us that this wish to have just a little more is unending. No matter how much money we have, how big a home we have or how nice a car we have, we always want just a little more.

CHANAKYA ON GREED

Chanakya too asserts that greed and thirst are similar. Chapter 14 of *Chanakya Niti* states, 'A man regrets upon his act of sin after accomplishing it. If the same wisdom is shown before performing the action, then the man will definitely attain Nirvana.'

We need to stop and think when we are feeling greedy or thirsty. Think of past situations involving greed and you will realize that greed targets our inefficiency or unwillingness to make accurate decisions, exploiting the instinctive desire within us to gain something that is normally not ours.

Chanakya goes on to suggest a three-step process for overcoming greed:

1. Use logic: A wise person asks questions and proceeds only after getting a satisfactory answer.
2. Self-control: We need to be responsible towards ourselves. We must have control over our cravings. We must not allow anything to sabotage our decision.
3. Follow dharma: Be good and do the right thing.

When we are controlled by our desires and our greed, our mind loses focus. We chase after something or the other

that is not relevant in our lives. More often than not, once we get what we were looking for, we wonder whether the entire effort was worth it.

I have addressed anger separately in the next section while I have discussed greed above; I will now explore the other forms of negative influences, which are lust, delusion (ego) and jealousy.

∞

The *Mahabharata* has several examples of the impact of negative influences on different characters in the epic. We can draw lessons from these examples as we face similar challenges every day in our lives.

1. King Shantanu was blinded by his love for Satyavati. Satyavati's father accepted the match on the condition that Satyavati's son would succeed Shantanu. It was this condition that led Bhishma to pledge that he would never marry and not stake his claim to the throne.
2. The blind King Dhritarashtra, because of his love for his son Duryodhana, refused to give the Pandavas their due. He rationalized this based on his belief that he was cheated out of the throne despite him being the older brother, simply because he was blind.
3. Yudhishthira, driven by his interpretation of dharma, accepted Dhritarashtra's invitation to gamble. Once he started to lose everything, greed overtook him and he decided to gamble his brothers and Draupadi in the faint hope that he could win back his kingdom.
4. Duryodhana asked Shakuni to roll the dice knowing that his uncle was a skilled gambler. But Shakuni's motive

was different. He wanted to take revenge on the blind Dhritarashtra who had married his sister Gandhari. Despite outwardly expressing love for his nephew, Shakuni's true motive was to destroy Hastinapur.
5. Draupadi was angry after Yudhishthira lost her to Duryodhana while gambling. She vowed not to tie her hair till it was washed with blood from the heart of Duryodhana's brother Dushasana. Bhima swore that he would to fulfil this vow by tearing open Dushasana's chest. Bhima also pledged to break Duryodhana's thigh because he had asked Draupadi to sit on his lap.
6. After Guru Dronacharya died, his son Ashwatthama vowed to take revenge and kill the five Pandava brothers. Late at night, he slipped into their tent and mistakenly killed the five sons of the Pandavas instead. Krishna cursed Ashwatthama with eternal life and it is said that he still walks this Earth, looking for release from the curse.

There are stories of greed, lust and revenge in the *Ramayana* as well. Unlike the *Mahabharata* where the battle was for a Kingdom, the *Ramayana* has stories of personal greed.

1. Kaikeyi wanted the kingdom for her son Bharata, who was younger than Rama. When King Dasharatha refused, she called upon the two promises the King had granted her earlier. She asked for the kingdom for her son and the banishment of Rama from the kingdom for 14 years.
2. Shurpanakha, Ravana's sister, was so enamoured with Lord Rama that she insisted that Ravana capture Rama and give him to her.
3. Kumbhakarna, Ravana's brother, prayed to Lord Brahma,

who was pleased and told Kumbhakarna that he could ask for any boon. Kumbhakarna decided that we would ask for *Indrasana* (the throne of Lord Indra). Saraswati, the Goddess of Learning, at the request of Lord Indra, ensured that when Kumbhakarna asked for his boon, the words that came out of his mouth were *Nidrasana* (the desire to sleep), which resulted in him sleeping for 6 months every year.

MANAGEMENT MANTRAS

As a manager, it is essential to understand the various negative influences that can impact the minds of employees. These influences can result in decreased productivity, reduced job satisfaction and can even lead to burnout. We will now discuss several negative influences on the mind and their effects on employees.

Workplace stress is one of the most common negative influences on the mind. It can result from various factors such as high workload, tight deadlines, insufficient resources and conflicts with colleagues. When employees experience prolonged stress, it can result in physical and mental health problems, including anxiety, depression and burnout. It can also affect the quality of work, leading to decreased productivity and job satisfaction.

To mitigate the effects of workplace stress, managers need to create a positive work environment that fosters support and understanding. This can involve providing employees with resources and tools to manage their workload, setting realistic expectations and deadlines and promptly addressing conflicts. Regular communication with employees to understand their concerns and offer support can also help to reduce stress levels.

In today's digital age, employees are constantly connected to their work through technology, which can result in information overload, heightened stress levels and feelings of being overwhelmed. Further, the constant need to be connected to work can erode work–life balance, leading to burnout and decreased job satisfaction.

To combat the effects of technology overload, managers can encourage employees to disconnect from work and prioritize self-care. They can also implement policies to limit after-hour emails and other forms of communication and provide employees with the tools to manage their workload efficiently.

When employees feel that their opinions and ideas are not valued, this too can result in a lack of motivation and decreased job satisfaction. Employees who lack autonomy in their work often feel demotivated and disengaged. A lack of autonomy can also lead to feelings of boredom and burnout, as employees are not able to take ownership of their work and innovate.

To enhance employee engagement and job satisfaction, managers can empower employees by giving them autonomy in their work. This can involve allowing employees to take ownership of their work, encouraging creativity and recognizing and rewarding innovative ideas. Managers can also offer training and development opportunities to help employees acquire new skills and knowledge.

Poor leadership can have a significant impact on employee morale and job satisfaction. When employees do not trust or respect their leaders, it can result in feelings of disengagement and apathy towards work. Poor leadership can also lead to conflicts and create a toxic work environment that is damaging to employees' mental health.

To improve leadership, managers can seek feedback from employees and take a proactive approach to address any issues. They can also work on developing their leadership skills and create a culture of trust and respect within the organization. Regular communication and recognition of employee contributions can also help to build trust and foster a positive work environment.

Negative influences on the mind can have a profound impact on employee morale, productivity and job satisfaction. As a manager, it is essential to understand these influences and take steps to address them. This can involve creating a positive work environment, empowering employees and improving leadership. By taking these steps, managers can improve employee well-being and foster a positive and productive workplace culture.

MANAGING ANGER

मन: प्रकोपं रक्षेद् मनसा संवृत: स्यात्।
मनोदुश्चरितं हित्वा मनसा सुचरितं चरेत्।।

Conquer anger with non-anger.
Conquer wickedness with goodness.
Conquer miserliness with liberality.
Conquer a liar with truthfulness.

—*Dhammapada, Verse 233*

When Lord Rama and his army reached the shores of the country on their way to rescue Sita, they needed to build a bridge over the sea that would allow the army to cross over to Lanka. The sea was rough and all their efforts of building a bridge were being washed away. Rama requested Varuna, the God of the Sea, to allow them to build the bridge but he did not agree. After three days of futile attempts, Rama became angry and asked Lakshmana to bring his bow and arrow so that he could dry up the waters of the sea for his army's safe passage through the bed of sand. Varuna understood the ramifications and pleaded for mercy.

The above incident from the *Ramayana* highlights that even Lord Rama, who is normally associated with peace, calmness and patience, got angry.

Anger is one of the most common and frequent emotions we experience. It manifests in us in different forms. Our anger could range from mild and moderate irritability to destructive aggression and uncontrollable rage. There are many theories regarding why we experience anger but the most common is that anger is a part of our survival and defence mechanisms.

We live in an angry society, comprising desk rage, road rage, domestic violence, spousal abuse, child abuse, sports rage, spam rage and more recently pandemic rage. Very few people are comfortable with their anger and dislike those who are prone to frequent bouts of anger.

LORD KRISHNA TOO GETS ANGRY

Shishupala, Krishna's cousin brother, had three eyes and four arms, and a prophecy foretold that his body would return to normal if held by the one destined to end his life. It so happened that when Krishna held his brother in his arms, Shishupala became normal.

Shishupala's mother then pleaded with Krishna to not kill his cousin, to which he replied that he would forgive the first 100 sins committed by Shishupala.

When they grew up, Shishupala's close friend Rukmi wanted the former to marry his sister Rukmini, but she chose to elope with Krishna. This angered Shishupala and he started treating Krishna as his enemy.

Several years later, Yudhishthira organized a *yagna* where it was decided that Krishna would be the first honoured guest. This angered Shishupala and he started abusing Krishna. When people tried to stop him, Krishna asked them to let him speak. Once Shishupal crossed his 100-abuse limit, Krishna beheaded him with his Sudarshana Chakra.

Anger is thus impulsive and could push us to act quickly and irrationally. Anger impairs our judgment, just as the morning haze obscures the skyline. We commit mistakes when we are angry and have regrets later. Sometimes the damage has already been done.

∞

There is another interesting story from the Mahabharata that demonstrates how a calm mind can win over someone's anger.

After Bhima, Arjuna, Nakula and Sahadeva died as a result of not listening to the yaksha in the *Mahabharata*, Yudhishthira was asked to answer a set of questions to resurrect his brothers.

The yaksha asked Yudhishthira, 'What is it that, by renouncing, makes a man dear to others? What is it which if given up never leads to misery? What is it which if renounced leads to wealth? And what is it which if renounced leads to happiness?'

Yudhishthira responded, 'Giving up pride makes a person dearer to others. Abandoning anger never leads to misery. Desire, if renounced, makes one wealthy. And the abandonment of avarice leads to happiness.'

Yudhishthira was able to please the yaksha with his answers and his four brothers were given their life back.

∞

As we grow older, we begin to understand the need to give up negativity. Our negativity towards people or actions only impacts ourselves. No one else is bothered or impacted by our negativity, except possibly our immediate family who may be affected because of their proximity to us.

Our scriptures have discussed anger and its consequences several times. Even our Gods and Rishis experienced anger from time to time. The result of their anger was usually a curse (of course, when they were happy, they did grant boons).

There are some well-known examples of when rishis and other enlightened people got angry:

1. When Rishi Bhrigu visited Kailasha to meet Lord Shiva, he was stopped by Nandi as the divine couple were engaged intimately. An enraged Bhrigu cursed Shiva that he would, henceforth, be worshipped as the *lingam* (male reproductive organ).
2. Parashurama taught the art of war to Bhishma and Dronacharya. He also bestowed the knowledge of Brahmastra upon Karna, thinking that Karna was a Brahmin. When he realized that Karna had lied to him, Parshurama cursed him saying that Karna would forget the knowledge of the Brahmastra when he needed it the most.
3. Parshurama went to Mount Kailash to pay his obeisance to Lord Shiva but Ganesha stopped him. This angered Parshurama and he started fighting Ganesha. During the fight, Parshurama threw his axe at Ganesha, thus breaking one of the tusks of Ganesha.
4. Rishi Durvasa was famous for his temper. One day, Durvasa was eating *kheer* (milk pudding) in the presence of Lord Krishna and ordered Krishna to apply the leftover *kheer* to his body. Krishna applied it on Durvasa's body but did not put any on his feet. Durvasa got angry at this seeming oversight and cursed Krishna, 'Since you did not obey my orders and did not apply the *kheer* on my feet, then your feet will be vulnerable to harm.' It is well known that Krishna eventually died because a hunter's arrow struck his foot.

Lord Krishna also speaks of anger several times in the *Gita*:

1. ध्यायतो विषयान्पुंसः सङ्गस्तेषूपजायते।
   सङ्गात्सञ्जायते कामः कामात्क्रोधोऽभिजायते।।
   —*Bhagavad Gita, Chapter 2, Verse 62*

   A person dwelling on sense objects develops an attachment to them, and from such attachment springs unfulfilled desire, which leads to anger.

2. क्रोधाद्भवति सम्मोहः सम्मोहात्स्मृतिविभ्रम।
   स्मृतिभ्रंशाद् बुद्धिनाशो बुद्धिनाशात्प्रणश्यति।।
   —*Bhagavad Gita, Chapter 2, Verse 63*

   Anger leads to delusion, which results in confusing memories. This bewilderment destroys our intellect. When our intellect is destroyed, we are as good as ruined.

3. वीतरागभयक्रोधा मन्मया मामुपाश्रिता।
   बहवो ज्ञानतपसा पूता मद्भावमागता।।
   —*Bhagavad Gita, Chapter 4, Verse 10*

   After freeing the self from attachment, fear and anger, followed by being completely absorbed and taking refuge in Me, a person can be purified with cosmic knowledge and thus attain a Godlike nature.

4. शक्नोतीहैव यः सोढुं प्राक्शरीरविमोक्षणात्।
   कामक्रोधोद्भवं वेगं स युक्तः स सुखी नरः।।
   —*Bhagavad Gita, Chapter 5, Verse 23*

   If one can withstand the combined forces of desire and anger, only that person is happy in this world.

5. श्रीभगवानुवाच।
    अभयं सत्त्वसंशुद्धिर्ज्ञानयोगव्यवस्थिति।
    दानं दमश्च यज्ञश्च स्वाध्यायस्तप आर्जवम्।।
    अहिंसा सत्यमक्रोधस्त्याग: शान्तिरपैशुनम्।
    दया भूतेष्वलोलुप्त्वं मार्दवं ह्रीरचापलम्।
    तेज: क्षमा धृति: शौचमद्रोहोनातिमानिता।
    भवन्ति सम्पदं दैवीमभिजातस्य भारत।।

    —*Bhagavad Gita, Chapter 16, Verses 1–3*

Lord Krishna describes 26 saintly virtues that we should pursue to elevate ourselves—lack of fear, purity of mind, steadfastness in spiritual knowledge, charity, controlling our senses, sacrifice, self-studying the sacred books, austerity and straightforwardness; non-violence, truthfulness, absence of anger, renunciation of our pride, peacefulness, not condemning anyone, compassion towards all living beings, lack of attachment, tenderness, modesty and lack of fickleness; vigour, forgiveness, courage, cleanliness, enmity towards no one and lack of pride.

∞

Several instances of anger can also be observed in the *Mahabharata*:

1. King Pandu, the foster father of the five Pandava brothers, accidentally shot Rishi Kindama when he was in the form of a deer that was mating. The rishi appeared in his human form and with his dying breath cursed Pandu that he would die the moment he approached one of his wives with the intent of making love. Pandu was

careful but forgot about the curse one day; he met his demise while engaging in intercourse with his younger wife Madri.

2. Gandhari, when she saw her son Duryodhana lying on the ground, his thighs broken by Bhima, was distraught. All 100 of her sons were either dead or dying. She was angry with Yudhishthira for not following the path of dharma and was about to curse him when Krishna intervened. Gandhari redirected her anger at Krishna.

   Gandhari's anger towards Krishna is a complex emotion rooted in her maternal love and her sense of duty. She blames Krishna for not preventing the war and for the loss of her sons, whom she loved deeply despite their flawed characters.

   It is crucial to recognize that Gandhari's anger is not one-dimensional. It is layered with grief, frustration and a sense of injustice. She represents the human aspect of the *Mahabharata*, where emotions are often in conflict with the principles of dharma. Her anger serves as a reminder that even in the face of divine intervention and guidance, human emotions and suffering cannot be easily quelled.

3. Karna had lived his entire life as the son of a charioteer, a *sutaputra*. When he died, Kunti, mother of the Pandavas, disclosed that Karna was her firstborn from an alliance with the Sun God, and that she had not been able to keep Karna because she was not married. Yudhishthira, on realizing that Karna was his older brother and should have inherited the Kingdom, cursed all women that henceforth they would not be able to keep any secrets.

∞

Anger, according to *Srimad Bhagavatam*, is generally considered a negative emotion that can lead to destructive consequences if not controlled. Here are some teachings and insights from *Srimad Bhagavatam* on anger:

1. Controlling anger: Individuals need to control their anger. Uncontrolled anger can cloud one's judgment and lead to harmful actions.
2. Anger as an enemy: Anger is depicted as an enemy of the self. It is compared to a destructive force that can harm not only the person who is angry but also those around them.
3. Devotion and surrender: Developing a deep sense of devotion and surrender to the Divine can help individuals manage their anger.
4. Forgiveness and compassion: Forgiveness and compassion are considered to be antidotes to anger. Practising forgiveness and showing kindness to those who provoke anger can help alleviate its negative effects.
5. Wisdom and discrimination: Individuals are advised to cultivate wisdom and discrimination to deal with situations that trigger anger.
6. Detachment: Detachment from material desires and attachments is a strong way to control anger. When one is less attached to worldly possessions and outcomes, there is a reduced likelihood of anger being triggered.

∞

ANGER IN BUDDHISM

In Buddhist teachings, anger is most often metaphorically compared to either an 'out of control forest fire' or a 'rampaging elephant'. Why these two? Simply because anger reacts and destroys quickly. We often do not have time to control our anger—angry words that hurt, angry fists that bruise, angry weapons that kill, angry actions that destroy relationships and angry reactions that destroy business deals.

It is worth remembering the story of Buddha calming the 'rampaging elephant' with a simple gesture and a peaceful demeanour. The teachings of the Buddha recommend the following solutions for anger management:

1. Meditate mindfully in the present moment; observe anger but do not participate.
2. Be attentive to the kindness of others and overlook their unkindness.
3. Practise loving-kindness and compassion for all beings, and put your enemies first during your meditation.
4. Use wisdom and patience; meditatively analyse anger and understand its cause and effect. Approach problems with patience and you will notice that with time, anger fades.
5. Substitute something positive for the negative. If someone's action angers you, analyse the person to find the positives you can focus on.

Different people react differently to the same event. Some people recover much more quickly than others when provoked by any negative emotion. Anger can be managed best through a process of self-realization. When we are angry, nothing and no one matters. When we recover from the anger, we wonder what made us angry and more often than not, we regret our outbursts.

We can easily recognize when we are getting angry and there are several techniques available to manage our growing anger, the first one being to retreat or walk away. This is easier said than done but if we are aware and conscious and if we decide to make the effort because of our self-awareness, our battle with anger would have been won.

We should know that it is time to retreat when we are:

- feeling overwhelmed during an argument,
- raising our voice to an unusual level,
- feeling our temper is getting out of control,
- experiencing elevated heartbeat,
- sensing our muscles tensing and
- starting to feel hostile.

Temporarily removing ourselves from the situation allows our body to return to our normal state and lets our brain reason and think logically.

This also prevents us from saying things in the heat of the moment that we might regret later. Walking away as an option works if we choose this as an option. Counselling the other party to 'walk away' from an argument may not be a path to take in the heat of the moment. While walking away, it is also a good idea to state that you are walking away because you need time to think about the discussion that has resulted in the argument, leading to anger.

Human emotions, including anger, don't arise out of a vacuum. They are typically a reaction to an external stimulus or an internal thought process. When someone is angry, it's usually in response to an event, a situation, a person's actions, memories or even fears and insecurities. While anger always has a reason, the justification for that anger might not always be sound, constructive or rational.

Here are a few reasons why:

1. Impulsive reactions: Humans sometimes react impulsively to situations without fully processing them. This can result in anger that, upon reflection, might seem unwarranted or excessive.
2. Misunderstandings: Many times, anger arises from miscommunications or misconceptions. If people took the time to communicate and understand each other better, many of these instances of anger might be avoided.
3. Misplaced anger: This is when someone is angry about one thing but takes it out on someone or something else.
4. Exaggerated responses: Sometimes, individuals might have an exaggerated emotional response due to past traumas or experiences. What seems like a minor trigger to one person could be significant to someone else because of their personal history.
5. Cultural or societal conditioning: In some cultures or societies, showing anger might be a way of asserting dominance or control. Such expressions of anger might not be based on genuine grievances but on the desire to maintain a certain image or power dynamics.

While it is natural and human to feel anger, one should introspect and evaluate whether the reasons for that anger are valid and constructive. Responding rather than reacting, seeking clarity and practising empathy can often reduce unnecessary anger and its associated negative consequences.

MANAGEMENT MANTRAS

Anger can be defined as a natural and often automatic response to a perceived threat or challenge. It is an emotional state that ranges from mild annoyance to intense rage and can be triggered by a wide range of events such as frustration, injustice and disappointment. While anger can be a helpful emotion that motivates individuals to take action, it can also be destructive when it leads to impulsive or irrational behaviour.

Thus, anger management is a critical aspect of life, especially for those in leadership positions, as leaders are responsible for overseeing the work of others, making decisions and handling conflicts. For managers, anger management is crucial because they often face stressful situations that can trigger intense feelings of frustration and anger.

As a manager, one must be able to control their emotions, maintain a professional demeanour and handle situations that may trigger anger in a rational and controlled manner. For example, managers may have to deal with difficult employees, make tough decisions or handle challenging customers. If they are not able to manage their anger, they can lose control, become irrational and make impulsive decisions that can have negative consequences.

Moreover, as leaders, managers set an example for others, and their behaviour can have a significant impact on their employees. If a manager demonstrates poor anger management skills, it can create a hostile work environment, lower morale and lead to decreased productivity. In contrast, a manager who demonstrates effective anger management skills can foster a positive and supportive workplace culture, improve employee morale and increase productivity.

One effective method for managing anger is to identify and understand the triggers that cause anger. This can involve analysing past experiences, reflecting on how one typically responds to challenging situations and being aware of specific events or circumstances that typically lead to anger. Once a manager has identified their triggers, they can develop strategies to manage their emotions, such as taking deep breaths, practising mindfulness, or engaging in physical activity.

Another critical aspect of anger management is communication. Managers must be able to communicate their feelings in a calm and controlled manner. They should avoid aggressive behaviour and instead focus on expressing their opinions and concerns in a non-threatening way. This can involve using 'I' statements instead of blaming others, staying calm and rational and avoiding impulsive behaviour.

Managers can also benefit from using problem-solving techniques to manage anger. For example, they can identify the cause of the problem and determine possible solutions. This can involve seeking the perspectives of others and considering multiple options before making a decision. Additionally, managers can also seek support from colleagues or engage in therapy or counselling to develop effective anger management strategies.

In conclusion, anger management is essential for managers in today's fast-paced and demanding workplace.

It is crucial for maintaining a positive and productive work environment, setting an example for others and avoiding negative consequences. Effective anger management strategies can include identifying triggers, communicating calmly and using problem-solving techniques. By developing and implementing these strategies, managers can increase their emotional intelligence and become more effective leaders.

LESSONS FROM HANUMAN

बुद्धिहीन तनु जानिके, सुमिरौं पवन-कुमार।
बल बुद्धि विद्या देहु मोहिं, हरहु कलेस बिकार।।

Knowing my body to be devoid of intelligence,
I remember Hanuman, the son of the wind-god.
Bestow upon me strength, intelligence, and knowledge,
and remove all ailments and impurities.

—*Hanuman Chalisa, Couplet 2*

Hanuman is the son of Vayu, the Hindu God of the Winds.

While he is a central character in the *Ramayana*, he is also mentioned in several other texts, such as the *Mahabharata* and various Puranas. In the *Mahabharata*, at the request of Lord Krishna, he agrees to sit on the flag of Arjuna's chariot. It is believed that with Hanuman on the flag, Arjuna's chariot got the stability that was needed with Lord Krishna as his charioteer (*sarathi*).

Lord Rama had great respect and admiration for Hanuman. He recognized Hanuman's unwavering devotion, bravery and selflessness, often praising him for his noble qualities.

One of the most well-known instances is when Hanuman helped with Sita's rescue from the clutches of Ravana. Hanuman used his extraordinary powers to cross the ocean and reach Lanka. He encountered various challenges along the way but he never lost faith in Lord Rama and his mission.

When Hanuman finally found Sita, he was so moved by her sorrow and loneliness that he wanted to bring her back to Lord Rama immediately. Hanuman's bravery and strength in battle impressed Lord Rama, who praised him for his courage and determination. Lord Rama said, 'You are indeed a great warrior, Hanuman. Your unwavering devotion to me and Sita is an inspiration to us all.'

Lord Rama also praised Hanuman's intelligence and wisdom. Hanuman was known for his quick thinking and problem-solving skills in difficult situations. He used his intelligence and wisdom to help Lord Rama and his army during the battle against Ravana. Lord Rama said, 'You are a wise and intelligent warrior, Hanuman. Your ability to think quickly and find solutions in difficult situations is truly remarkable.'

In addition to his bravery and intelligence, Lord Rama also praised Hanuman for his humility and selflessness. Hanuman never sought recognition or reward for his actions and always put the needs of others before his own. Lord Rama said, 'You are a true servant of the Gods, Hanuman. Your selflessness and humility are a shining example of the kind of person we should all strive to be.'

Lord Rama's admiration for Hanuman is also evident in his praise for the latter's compassion and kindness. Despite his great power and strength, Hanuman never used it to harm others and always acted with compassion and kindness. Lord Rama said, 'You are a true embodiment of love and compassion, Hanuman. Your kindness and gentle spirit are a testament to your noble character.'

Lord Rama recognized that Hanuman was a true servant of the Gods and a shining example of what it means to be noble and virtuous. Lord Rama's praise for Hanuman serves as a reminder of the importance of these qualities in our own lives and inspires us to strive for the same level of devotion, bravery, intelligence, humility and kindness that Hanuman displayed.

Lord Krishna too had a lot to say about Hanuman, and his teachings offer valuable lessons for all of us:

1. Lord Krishna considered Hanuman to be the epitome of devotion, as he was completely devoted to Lord Rama and always acted in his best interest. Lord Krishna stated that when we are completely devoted to a higher power, we gain immense strength and wisdom, enabling us to overcome obstacles and achieve our goals. He said that devotion is not just about offering prayers and gifts, but about being fully dedicated to the cause and acting with selflessness.

2. Lord Krishna also considered Hanuman to be a true embodiment of selflessness as he put the needs of others before his own and was always willing to help others. He said that when we put the needs of others before our own, we become more humble, compassionate and

virtuous. Selflessness is not just a virtue but a key to happiness and fulfilment in life.
3. Lord Krishna highlighted that Hanuman represents the power of courage and bravery, as the latter was never afraid to face any danger or obstacle in order to serve Lord Rama. He was courageous and showed strength even in the face of danger. Lord Krishna said that when we have the courage to stand up for our beliefs, even in the face of opposition, we become stronger and more confident. Hanuman taught that courage is not only about facing physical danger but also about standing up for our values and beliefs in the face of challenges and obstacles.

These teachings inspire a holistic approach to life, integrating devotion, selflessness and courage for a fulfilling journey.

MANAGEMENT MANTRAS

Hanuman, known for his devotion and unwavering loyalty to Lord Rama, holds valuable lessons for modern-day managers and leaders. His life story, as depicted in the *Ramayana*, serves as a model for leadership, teamwork and strategic thinking.

Let us examine the management lessons that can be gleaned from Hanuman's character and actions.

Leadership

One of the key management lessons from Hanuman is the importance of leadership. Throughout the *Ramayana*, Hanuman displays several leadership qualities, such as courage, determination and the ability to inspire others. He is able to rally his troops and lead them in their mission to find Sita.

In modern management, leaders must possess the same qualities that Hanuman displayed. Courage is an essential quality for leaders, as they must be able to make difficult decisions and stand by them even in the face of opposition. Hanuman's determination proved critical as it allowed him to overcome obstacles and never give up on his mission to find Sita. Leaders must inspire their employees, just as Hanuman inspired his troops.

By providing direction, support and a clear vision, leaders can motivate their employees to achieve their goals.

Teamwork

Another management lesson from Hanuman is the importance of teamwork. Throughout his journey, Hanuman relies on the support and cooperation of his fellow soldiers and allies. For example, when Hanuman reaches Lanka, he forms a team of monkeys to help him in his mission to find Sita. This teamwork allows him to overcome obstacles and complete his mission successfully.

In modern-day management, teamwork is just as critical as it was for Hanuman. Teams that work together effectively can achieve far greater results than individuals working alone. Leaders must cultivate a culture of collaboration and encourage their employees to work together to achieve their goals. By fostering teamwork, managers can increase productivity, reduce stress and improve employee morale.

Strategic Thinking

Hanuman is also an excellent strategic thinker. Hanuman uses his wit and intelligence to overcome obstacles and achieve his goals. For example, when he encounters a vast ocean that separates him from Lanka, he quickly comes up with a plan to cross it by growing in size and using his strength to jump across the ocean.

In modern management, strategic thinking is just as important as it was for Hanuman. Leaders must be able to analyse situations and make decisions that will help their organization achieve its goals. They must be able to think critically and creatively to find solutions to problems and overcome obstacles. By developing their strategic thinking skills, managers can ensure that their organizations are always moving forward and adapting to changing circumstances.

Devotion

Another management lesson from Hanuman is the importance of devotion. Throughout the *Ramayana*, Hanuman demonstrates a deep and unwavering devotion to Lord Rama, which drives him to complete his mission and helps him overcome the many challenges he faces along the way.

In modern management, devotion to a cause or mission can be just as important. Leaders must be passionate about their work and dedicated to achieving their goals. They must be able to inspire their employees to share their vision and work together to achieve their mission. By fostering a culture of devotion and commitment, leaders can ensure that their employees are always motivated to work towards their goals.

ANAHATA CHAKRA

Emotional Intelligence and Accountability

The fourth is the Anahata or the Heart Chakra, seen as a gateway to higher consciousness. When balanced, it helps individuals navigate life's challenges with a calm and centred approach, encouraging open and honest expression while considering the feelings and perspectives of others. Emotional intelligence resonates in ancient Hindu scriptures, notably the *Bhagavad Gita*, which underscores the significance of self-awareness, self-regulation and empathy. Lord Krishna stresses managing our desires and emotions to achieve inner calm, aligning with the components of emotional intelligence, namely, self-awareness and self-regulation. The Vedas, Upanishads and other texts emphasize empathy and compassion, integral facets of emotional intelligence. The concept of '*Atman*' or inner self highlights introspection, a core element of emotional intelligence. Essentially, Hindu scriptures offer profound insights into understanding and mastering our emotional realm.

Accountability means taking responsibility and being answerable to ourselves for our actions. When we are accountable for our actions, we demonstrate integrity and a commitment to ethical behaviour.

Honesty is the foundation of ethical behaviour and is essential for promoting trust and accountability. Corruption, in contrast, is a violation of trust and a betrayal of ethical behaviour.

Ego is closely related to honesty and corruption. Ego is the belief in our own superiority, and it can lead to a sense of entitlement and a disregard for ethical behaviour. Ego is a major obstacle to spiritual and moral growth.

Ethics are the principles that guide individuals' behaviour and decision-making. Our scriptures emphasize the importance of compassion, non-violence and truthfulness.

Trust is the foundation of all relationships, including personal and professional. Trust is built on honesty, consistency and reliability, and is essential for creating a stable and supportive community.

Emotional intelligence, accountability, honesty, corruption, ego, ethics and trust are concepts that have been prevalent in our scriptures for thousands of years. By cultivating emotional intelligence, individuals can develop empathy, compassion and self-awareness, which are essential for building trust and promoting honesty.

HONESTY AND CORRUPTION

> It is impossible to know when
> and how much water a fish drinks.
> Similar is the act of officials stealing government money.
>
> —*Chanakya Niti*

Chanakya believed in employing spies and whistle-blowers to keep a check on officials to ensure that they performed their work properly. They were provided awards and incentives to expose corruption.

The most famous whistle-blower is probably Vibhishana, the younger brother of Ravana. When Lord Rama was unable to kill Ravana, Vibhishana told Lord Rama the secret of Ravana's long life. On getting this information, Lord Rama was able to kill Ravana. The *Mahabharata* has other examples as well where Lord Krishna provides Arjuna and Bhima with the secrets of slaying Bhishma and Duryodhana in the war, respectively.

Instances of insiders calling out corruption and unethical behaviour take place all the time. Employees are often confronted with a huge ethical dilemma: How does a worker know what warrants a whistle-blower response? Anyone facing the question knows that they take the risk of being portrayed as an alarmist or disloyal on the one hand or tacitly approving of illegal or unethical activity on the other. The employee has to make the ethical decision of whether there is in fact wrongdoing, and whether the wrongdoing is so severe that it outweighs any duties of loyalty they have to the organization on the ethical scale.

But the price in many organizations for blowing the whistle can be high, ranging from being socially ostracized to being fired in retaliation. Making an accusation can indeed transform workplace relationships.

Ethical leadership is thus an important factor influencing a worker's decision on whether to report an ethical transgression. Employees look for social cues on whether to blow the whistle.

∞

Corruption has been a matter of discussion and debate since time immemorial. As long as there are human beings, there will be corruption. Corruption could be defined as the abuse of entrusted power for private gain. It could be for financial benefit, political power, religious beliefs and any matter that affects our lives as human beings. It erodes trust, weakens democracy, hampers economic development and further exacerbates inequality, poverty, social division and the environmental crisis. Exposing corruption and holding the corrupt to account can only happen if we understand the way corruption works and the systems that enable it.

Our scriptures themselves often extol virtues and righteous living but they also shed light on the human frailties, vices and corruption.

Corruption is represented in various forms:

1. Political corruption in the *Mahabharata*: The game of dice, wherein Yudhishthira loses his kingdom and his wife Draupadi is humiliated, is a stark representation of deceit and political manipulation.
2. Moral corruption in the *Ramayana*: The kidnapping

of Sita by Ravana underscores the perils of unchecked desire and the violation of moral codes.
3. Deviations from dharma: When individuals or societies deviate from dharma, it can be seen as a form of corruption. This is evident in numerous tales from the Puranas where Gods and mortals deviate from their path.
4. Desire and greed in the *Gita*: Unchecked desires lead to anger and delusion, culminating in the degradation of one's memory and understanding, ultimately leading to one's spiritual ruin.
5. Power dynamics in the Puranas: Many stories reveal how the intoxication of power can lead Gods and demons alike to acts of corruption and tyranny.

Corruption in our scriptures is not portrayed merely as a historical or societal ill but is deeply woven into the existential and ethical fabric of human existence.

There are many stories of moral corruption arising out of greed in the Mughal times and during the British era. Greed, moral corruption, war and destruction have coexisted since the beginning of civilization. The insatiable desire for power has resulted in wars and battles of epic proportions.

From the Kurukshetra War of the *Mahabharata* to Lord Rama's battle with Ravana to bring Sita back; whether it be a blind father scheming and conniving to win the kingdom for his son or a mother coveting the throne for her son; from Hitler's actions in World War II to the conflict in Ukraine and from Kargil to Doklam, battles have been fought for territory and honour. These are some of the stories we have grown up listening to.

Yet, good finally conquers all in the end. There is bloodshed, pain and evil before the truth finally prevails.

Every generation refuses to learn from history. The futility of the power struggles and the accompanying corruption holds a lot of lessons for us. All experiential evidence shows that countries with the least corruption are the most progressive in terms of economic and sociological contexts.

We have learnt to accept a certain amount of corruption in our daily lives and this could be in any form. Every morning, many of us perform a 'trade with God'. If you give me something, I will donate something to Your place of worship, which is perfectly acceptable in most of our minds.

Corruption can be seen, amongst others, in the following forms:

- Bribery
- Embezzlement, theft and fraud
- Graft
- Extortion and blackmail
- Influence peddling
- Networking
- Abuse of discretion
- Favouritism, nepotism and clientelism

Corruption can include behaviours like:

- Public servants demanding or taking money or favours in exchange for services.
- Politicians misusing public money or granting public jobs or contracts to their sponsors, friends and families.
- Companies bribing officials to get lucrative deals.

Corruption can happen anywhere—in business, the government, judiciary, media and civil society, as well as across all sectors from health and education to infrastructure and sports. It can involve anyone, be it politicians, government officials, public servants, business persons or members of the public, all of whom are vulnerable to corruption.

Corruption takes place in the shadows, often with the help of professional enablers such as bankers, lawyers, accountants, real estate agents, opaque financial systems and anonymous shell companies, which allow corruption schemes to flourish and the corrupt to launder and hide their illicit wealth. Corruption adapts to different contexts and changing circumstances. It can evolve in response to changes in rules, legislation and even technology.

In my book *The Buck Stops Here*,[*] I have outlined an interesting set of interpretations and experiences related to honesty and corruption.

Laying the foundation of an honest organization—built with strong integrity and ethics—is important to set the culture, direction and priorities for any new company. The lead has to be taken by the leader of the company by setting the right example and standards for honesty.

Honesty is either black or white—there is no grey.

To me, honesty is a simple black-and-white subject. Neither is there any grey in honesty nor is there any shade of white and black as I have heard many people say. Either you are honest or you are dishonest.

---

[*]Garg, Ashutosh, *The Buck Stops Here*, Rupa Publications, New Delhi, 3 May 2014, 177.

I told both my sons when they were leaving home to pursue their education overseas that every morning when they are alone shaving and looking in the mirror, if they are able to look themselves in the eye and tell themselves, 'I did no wrong yesterday and I did not knowingly harm anyone yesterday', then that is the only explanation they would ever need to give to themselves. What anyone else thought of them or their actions was of no relevance and did not matter. My advice to my sons was as follows:

If someone doesn't like the way you handle something, hear them out, but you don't have to implement their idea. You can't please everyone.

THRESHOLD OF CONSCIENCE

As I progressed through my early working life, I began to understand that honesty had shades of grey and each person had their own threshold of conscience.

I have often argued with colleagues about whether using the company car to drop your children at school or to take your wife shopping or charging a personal expense as official entertainment or converting a business class ticket into two economy tickets when travelling overseas on official business so that your partner can fly for free is right or wrong. These are examples of when we alter our own threshold of conscience and accept a position that we would normally not accept for our colleagues. We would also not accept this as appropriate if we hear of someone else who has done something similar.

I learnt to accept that I am nobody to judge what is right and wrong on behalf of someone else because this is a pure value judgment call. As long as my own conscience is clear and as long as I know that I am doing what I think is right, I will keep moving forward.

I have always maintained my own sense of integrity, ethics and honesty in all my dealings as per my own threshold of conscience, though I know I have also learnt to look the other way if I see someone else following practices that I don't agree with.

A senior bureaucrat in a Southeast Asian country once told me that there was no corruption in his country. They believed in the philosophy of cooperation, not corruption. 'If you are going to do business in my country and make a profit, you need to cooperate and share a part of this profit with us', he said.[*]

Gifting is another area where several shades of grey with respect to honesty exist. In our country, there is a culture of exchanging gifts on Diwali every year and if a gift is not accepted, it is seen as an affront by the person giving the gift. Yet, if the person receiving the gift makes it abundantly clear that gifts aren't welcome, then the practice of exchanging gifts comes to a stop.

At Guardian, we used to receive a lot of gifts from our suppliers. Our policy was the same for all the gifts received; they must be received only at the Head Office of the company by the administrative department and logged. At the annual dinner of the company, we hold a lucky draw for all staff members and distribute these gifts. My name and the names of the management committee members are excluded from the lucky draw.

---

[*]Garg, Ashutosh, *The Buck Stops Here*, Rupa Publications, New Delhi, 3 May 2014, 175.

STANDARD OF HONESTY

Integrity, ethics and honesty can only be implemented in a company when the leader(s) set an example. It is also very important to set these standards from the very beginning.

If I had started a culture of taking free medicines from my company or asked the stores to send cash to me from the cash box or pulled cash out of the company, I would not have been able to demonstrate the right leadership on this value and there would have been no way for me to implement a strong value-based code of conduct in the company. To this day, I highlight every personal entertainment and other expense in my official credit card statement and every international personal phone call, paying for it separately from my own account.

∞

I clearly remember one incident from the early days of Guardian Pharmacy. I was standing near the cash counter of the first store of Guardian Pharmacy at Galleria Market in Gurugram, India. A well-dressed lady in her mid-thirties walked into the store and picked up some shampoos, soaps, cosmetics, health products and a few more items. She then walked up to the counter (I could see my behind-the-counter pharmacist colleague all excited because her total purchases would have then been a large part of our daily sales in our first store).

She put all these items on the counter, took out her credit card and said in a very matter-of-fact manner, 'Give me all these products but make a bill for antibiotic capsules and other medicines.'

The reason is that India's income tax laws permit ₹15,000 per year as a tax-free perquisite (medical reimbursement), provided appropriate medical bills are furnished. Most companies add this amount to their overall compensation package and in order to recover the 'tax-free' money that is a part of their total salary package, most individuals resort to submitting 'fake' bills.

My colleague knew my views on this but he still looked at me; I shook my head no. He could see the sale flying away but he responded, 'Sorry madam, at Guardian we can only give you a bill for what you purchase.'

This angered her and she started shouting at the store staff saying that she had never been to such a 'useless' store before and that her neighbourhood chemist always gave her a bill as per her requirements. She stormed out of the store in anger and we put the products back onto the store shelves. A few days later, she visited the store again and asked for some medicines. I walked up to her and said, 'Madam, we will not be able to give you a bill for anything other than what you have purchased.'

Her subsequent response was heart-warming and gave me the confidence that the path I was on was indeed the correct one for Guardian, 'If you don't give fake bills, I'm confident that you don't sell fake medicines', she said. She has been a loyal customer of Guardian ever since.

It is very difficult to say 'no' when you are confronted with an ethical issue but the cost of saying 'yes' will prove to be huge in the future. It is always better to say no now if you don't agree on a point than to suffer the consequences later.

This goes on to show that the real cause of corruption

and dishonesty is within us. Unless we root these out, we will continue to be corrupt.

MANAGEMENT MANTRAS

As managers, it is our responsibility to ensure that our organization runs efficiently and effectively and to provide a positive environment for our employees. A key aspect of this responsibility is to promote honesty and integrity within the workplace and prevent corruption.

Honesty is the foundation of trust, which is essential for creating a positive work environment and establishing good relationships between employees and managers. Honesty in the workplace is about being truthful and transparent in all business dealings, whether it be with clients, suppliers or co-workers. When employees and managers are honest, they foster a culture of trust and respect, which can lead to increased productivity and improved morale.

Corruption, in contrast, is a threat to both the stability and reputation of an organization. It can take any form, including bribery, embezzlement and fraud. Corruption undermines the values of the organization, erodes trust and destroys the morale of employees. It also has a negative impact on the wider community, reducing the quality of services and goods provided and reducing the level of investment in the organization.

As managers, we must take a proactive approach to prevent corruption within our organization. This means setting a clear standard of ethical behaviour and ensuring that employees understand what is expected of them. Managers should also promote transparency and accountability, and create an environment where employees feel comfortable reporting any instances of corruption that they may witness.

In addition, managers should be vigilant in detecting and reporting any suspicious behaviour and take appropriate action to ensure that any instances of corruption are thoroughly investigated and dealt with. This may involve implementing effective internal controls and ensuring that the necessary systems and procedures are in place to prevent and detect corruption.

Finally, managers should also lead by example, demonstrating honest and ethical behaviour in their own work practices. This will encourage employees to follow suit and create a culture of honesty and integrity within the workplace.

EGO

विहाय कामान्य: सर्वान्पुमांश्चरति नि:स्पृह:।
निर्ममो निरहङ्कार: स शान्तिमधिगच्छति।।

The person who gives up all material desires and lives a life that is free of greed, proprietorship and egoism attains peace

—*Bhagavad Gita, Chapter 2, Verse 71*

Most of the characters in the *Mahabharata*, barring Lord Krishna, had a huge ego. Duryodhana believed that after Dhritarashtra, he was the chosen one to be the King. Arjuna believed that he belonged to the best dynasty in the world and was the best archer. Bhima believed that he was the strongest person in the world and Karna believed that he was the best archer and was always looking for an opportunity to defeat Arjuna.

Draupadi had a huge ego, and this was demonstrated when Duryodhana fell into the water while walking around the new palace of the Pandavas and she called out 'the son of a blind person must be blind'. She took a vow not to tie her hair till it had been soaked in the blood of her brother-in-law Dushasana, who had wronged her.

Before the war started, both Arjuna and Duryodhana went to Lord Krishna to ask for his support. Lord Krishna was sleeping so Arjuna sat at his feet and Duryodhana sat next to his head. When Lord Krishna woke up, he saw Arjuna first and asked him what he wanted from him. Duryodhana immediately reacted, saying he was older and therefore deserved to be asked first. Lord Krishna agreed and Duryodhana asked for Lord Krishna's army. His ego made him forget who Lord Krishna was. In contrast, Arjuna asked Lord Krishna to be his charioteer or *sarathi*.

The ego, in its purest form, is identical to the self. Our scriptures equate our ego or aham with the Brahman. Aham or ego refers to the 'I' in each one of us.

Ahamkara is a Sanskrit word meaning 'I-making'. Its root word *aham* translates to 'self' and *kara* means 'doing' or 'acting'. Thus, ahamkara is the self that is doing or the personality associated with this individual body. It refers to the sense of being an individual separate from everything else. Ahamkara or the 'I' is the ego that enables us to develop a false sense of identity, which we believe to be true. In general, ahamkara has developed some negative connotations.

Our 'I' can often become unhealthy and distorted by thought patterns and incorrect beliefs that could lead to a feeling of separation, pain and suffering. It could create false identities and false perceptions of who we are. The mind creates a sense of being different from others and may result in our feeling separated or isolated. This could further lead to us not easily trusting others.

Our ahamkara could weaken us and make us suffer because it could be attached to people, places, things and ideas. It is the source behind our sense of I, me and mine and could lead to emotions like greed, anger, jealousy, hatred, pride, arrogance or selfishness. These emotions get inflamed when we do not get what we want.

Conversely, our ahamkara also has a strong positive side if we look at it from another perspective. We can use our ahamkara as a source of our willpower, commitment and determination to achieve the goals we have set for ourselves. We can harness the power of our ahamkara as a tool for personal growth.

When a person is overly proud and conceited, we say he has a lot of *aham*, meaning the person is egoistic.

When our mind functions positively, it protects us from any danger. It helps us to make the right decisions. We can take care of ourselves physically, emotionally, mentally, spiritually and financially. We also understand when we need to put others first by putting our own desires aside.

Our ahamkara helps us to take responsibility for our own lives and thus creates a sense of purpose and direction for ourselves.

The word '*aham*' appears in the *Bhagavad Gita* several times. It can be seen as a suffix in the following words:

- Agraham (anger)
- Dukham (sorrow)
- Sukham (happiness)
- Graham (grasping one)
- Purusham (individual self)

In each of these, we can see our self and how we interpret our self also depends on the state of our minds at that moment.

EVERYONE HAS AN EGO

Ego is a universal phenomenon; every human being has an ego. Our scriptures demonstrate that even our Gods have an ego.

Another way to look at ego is where we, through our self, attempt to demonstrate that we are different from others. Problems start when we attempt to show who we are not or try to project a false perception of ourselves.

Our ego manifests itself in various forms within us, which we then project to the outer world. These forms could be:

- Ownership
- Desire and attachment
- Pride and arrogance
- Self-esteem
- Selfishness
- Self-centredness
- Aggression and competitiveness
- Comparison
- Judgment, opinions and criticism
- Identification with the mind and body
- Fear, suffering, anxiety, anger, stress, etc.

In our lives, there is a 'real' us and the 'projected' us. The world knows us based on what we project but very few people know the 'real' us. Most of us hide our real selves behind a *mukhauta* or a mask. We do not want others to know the truth about us because, in our minds, we believe that such knowledge may make us vulnerable. Even after spending a lifetime with a person, in all probability, we may not know them inside out.

Our relationships, more often than not, are fragile. Our ego creates a barrier that prevents us from seeing the truth even about ourselves. It keeps us locked up in our minds.

EGO IS HARMFUL

Chanakya, after he was insulted and thrown out of the court of King Dhana Nanda, pledged that he would raise a King who would remove Dhana Nanda from the throne. To remind him of his pledge, he said that he would not tie his *shikha* or topknot till he had achieved his objective.

Ravana too had a huge ego. Through his penance, he had managed to gain a lot of celestial weapons. After he kidnapped Sita, he was repeatedly advised by his wife Mandodari and other elders that he should return Sita to Lord Rama with all respect and humility and seek forgiveness. Ravana was so convinced of his invincibility that he refused, only to meet his end at the hands of Lord Rama.

Taking a cue from these examples of ego that are present in our scriptures, we need to think of how we can manage our ego.

We need to ask ourselves the following questions:

1. Do we have trouble in working with our teams or do we find it difficult to ask for help from someone else?
2. Do we believe that other people do not seem to know anything as compared to ourselves? Are we so full of ourselves that we are not even willing to listen to sane advice from someone else?
3. Do we have problems in managing our relations with our peers, subordinates and superiors?

OVERCOMING OUR EGO

1. *Think of when you engage in turf wars*: Try a simple exercise. Sit with a colleague at a dining table facing each other. Move the salt and pepper shaker on the table towards your colleague without showing that you are doing this on purpose. Wait for their reaction. In all probability, your colleague will, in a few moments, move the salt and pepper shaker back to its original position. This is how each one of us manages our informally-defined turf. It is our ego that makes us behave the way we do.
2. *Stop comparing*: Comparisons are possibly the biggest deterrents for us to be satisfied. The greater the disparity in our minds, the bigger the hurt to our ego. The old example of a glass being half full versus half empty does not apply when it comes to managing our ego. The only way to stop comparing is when we start appreciating the other person more. If we must compare, then it is better to hold a mirror up to yourself and see how you are today compared to the previous day.
3. *Think of how you look at failure*: Most of us have been

taught to succeed all the time. Very few of us have been taught that 'it is okay to fail'. Failure can either have a very negative impact on our ego that may result in our not wanting to take any risks or it could spur us into taking action through our learnings from said failure. We need to learn to celebrate all our failures and if we are able to do this successfully, we would have taken a strong and decisive step towards managing our ego.

4. *Lower expectations from ourselves*: One of the biggest challenges that we face is the unreal expectations we place on ourselves. These are driven by our ego, where we believe that we have the ability to achieve the unachievable. Once we remove the trap of expectations that we are in, the burden that we are faced with also disappears. As children, we are often told that we have the power to achieve anything we want. There is absolutely nothing wrong with what our parents told us to motivate us. But in the workplace, we need to be more realistic about our strengths.

5. *Redefine success for ourselves*: In our work life, our performance is generally judged based on the next promotion or the size of the annual bonus. However, there are many other attributes of success that we need to be mindful of. It is a good practice to celebrate our successes, but it is even more important to celebrate the success of our colleagues.

6. *Understand the importance of compromise*: An important element in managing our ego is our ability to compromise. The importance of understanding the need to meet someone else's views in the 'middle' is very critical. If we reach a stalemate, we should relook at the

assumptions and if required, rethink these to meet the other person in the middle. Remove the friction that may be hindering our ability to arrive at a compromise.

7. *Encourage a difference of opinion*: Different opinions help team members to sharpen their perspectives. They also help to guide team members towards a unified goal. A difference of opinion needs to be encouraged all the time while remembering the cardinal rule that once a decision has been arrived at after factoring in multiple opinions, the team needs to close ranks and move forward together; there can be no room for disagreement once the team has taken a decision together. Another factor to remember is that we must not compromise our personal values, no matter how important it may be to seek a compromise.

8. *Demonstrate genuine interest in others*: We know when another person is genuinely interested in what we are saying. The same applies to us. We need to develop the simple skill of active listening. When we are talking to someone, we often see their eyes moving around the room, looking at others. The skill set that we need to develop is to show genuine interest when speaking or listening to someone else.

9. *Question yourself*: Being honest with oneself is the best test in any situation. Ask yourself two questions to understand your ego.
   a. Do I feel superior to others?
   b. Do I feel inferior to others?

   If the answer is 'yes' to either of these, our ego is probably a dominant part of our work, and realizing this will make all the difference in being able to take steps to manage our ego.

10. *Are you offended easily?*: An important factor in understanding our ego is if we get offended easily when someone holds a view that is in contrast to ours. People with large egos tend to assume that they have everything under control. Often, we do not even notice if we get offended easily.

Remember there is no 'I' in a team. Compromise should not mean defeat. Working with another person to achieve a goal while forfeiting something minor is worth it.

MANAGEMENT MANTRAS

Ego can play a significant role in the success or failure of a manager.

On the one hand, having a strong sense of self-confidence and self-esteem can help a manager make tough decisions, inspire their team and drive results. On the other hand, an overinflated ego can lead to arrogance, poor decision-making and strained relationships with team members and colleagues.

To be effective, a manager needs to strike a delicate balance between confidence and humility. A manager with a healthy ego understands their strengths and weaknesses and is willing to admit mistakes and learn from them. They lead by example, demonstrating a strong work ethic and a commitment to excellence, while also creating an environment that encourages open communication and collaboration.

However, when a manager's ego becomes too big, it can have negative consequences. An inflated ego can lead to a manager disregarding the opinions and ideas of others, making unilateral decisions without considering their impact on the team or organization as a whole. This can create a toxic work environment, foster resentment and disengagement among team members, and ultimately hurt the organization's overall performance.

In addition, an ego-driven manager may prioritize their own success over that of their team or organization. They may take credit for the successes of others or undermine their team members to maintain their own power and position. This type of behaviour not only harms team morale but also jeopardizes the manager's long-term success by eroding trust and respect.

Ego can be a double-edged sword for managers. While a healthy sense of self-confidence can be beneficial, an overinflated ego can be detrimental. Effective managers must strive to find a balance between confidence and humility and must put the needs of their team and organization ahead of their own success. By doing so, they can create a positive work environment, foster collaboration and drive results for their team and organization.

ETHICS

मयि क्रुद्धे जगन् स्यान्मयि सर्वं प्रतिष्ठितम्।
देवदानवगन्धर्वाः किंनरोरगराक्षसाः॥

Do naught unto others that would
cause you pain if done to you.

—*Mahabharata, Book 5, Chapter 15, Verse 17*

Maryada Purushottam Rama is the embodiment of dharma and ethical behaviour and there are several lessons we can draw from his life.

In contrast, Lord Krishna, in the *Mahabharata*, holds a different moral outlook. He urges the Pandavas to violate dharma and to deviate from the cosmic order. But for Him, conformity to the cosmic order and dharma is intrinsically good in the context of the setting of the *Mahabharata*.

As understood by each of us, ethics refers to concepts of good and evil based on our set of values, paradigms and relative context. It involves determining what is right or wrong based on personal perspectives. Ethical behaviour is commonly interpreted as comportment that adheres to a specific code of conduct recognized as authoritative in matters of morality.

Indic scriptures have laid the foundation for ethical and moral values that have stood the test of time. These scriptures encompass a wide range of philosophical, theological and moral insights, spanning the Vedas, Upanishads, *Bhagavad Gita*, *Ramayana*, *Mahabharata*, etc. At their core, they present a vision of life in which ethics plays a pivotal role, guiding human actions and ensuring harmony in society.

Religion plays an important part in the ethical decisions of most Hindus. For many, ethical behaviour is often seen as being necessary, both as an act of obedience to God's wishes and as a requirement for spiritual development.

Hindu ethics prescribe the norms that need to be observed consciously or unconsciously for as long as we live. It is based on the premise that ethical life is the means to spiritual freedom.

Ethics in Hinduism is personal, within a broadly-defined set of guidelines. Ethics is also seen as a part of dharma, related to our position in society and our stage in life. Hinduism also has certain universal ethical principles that apply to all human beings irrespective of their position in society or stage in life.

Central to the ethical discourse in Indic scriptures is the concept of 'Dharma'. Often translated as 'duty' or 'religion', Dharma is a multifaceted term that means righteousness, law and moral order. It is the guiding principle that dictates righteous living, emphasizing duties, rights, laws, conduct and virtues. Dharma sustains society, maintains social order and ensures well-being and progress of humanity.

Hindus are advised to control emotions like *kama* (lust), *krodha* (anger), *mada* (ego or pride) and *matsarya* (jealousy). We have discussed these emotions in a previous chapter.

LESSONS ON ETHICS

In the *Bhagavad Gita*, Lord Krishna states that the correctness of the action should be the primary consideration when doing something. He advises Arjuna to always act in accordance with dharma. He emphasizes selfless action and the performance of one's duty without attachment to the results. This is known as *nishkama karma*. This concept urges individuals to act ethically, without being swayed by personal gains or losses, thereby upholding the moral fabric of society. The teachings of the *Bhagavad Gita* are summed up in the words 'your business is with deed and not with the result'.

Dharmaraja Yudhishthira, the epitome of ethics, gambled away his kingdom, brothers and wife and then took all of them into the forest for 14 years. This has been explained not by the incorrect nature of gambling but by the fact that he lived up to his promise after losing in the game of dice. Once again, the context of the situation and not the act itself is important.

Eight virtues have been mentioned in the *Dharmasutras*, the guidebooks of Gautama Buddha. These are compassion, patience, contentedness, purity, earnest endeavour, pure thoughts, freedom from greed and freedom from envy.

Chanakya Niti outlines the following ethical qualities that should be present in every leader. For this book, we can take the meaning of a leader to be the leader of a business organization, a social grouping or a family.

- The leader is the face of the nation. They are responsible for everything that is happening in the community and hence are the society's reflection.
- The leader should work for the attainment of the common goal, which is the welfare of their people.
- The leader will lose the loyalty of their subjects if they dishearten them by their unjust actions.
- A leader should not propagate *adharma*, they should

not favour the wicked, should punish the culprit and should not punish the innocent.
- There should be no wasteful expenditure.
- An ethical leader should not antagonize the wise and their elders.
- They should hear all urgent matters of their subjects and should not postpone them, as justice delayed is justice denied.

We can also draw learnings on ethics from several scriptures and teachings including the Vedas, Upanishads and *Manusmriti*.

Ahimsa, or non-violence, is a cardinal virtue and an ethical foundation in Indic scriptures. Rooted in the belief that all life forms are interconnected, ahimsa promotes love, compassion and respect for all beings. The Upanishads and the Vedantic scriptures emphasize the unity of the soul with the cosmos. In this realization lies the foundation for ahimsa, as harming another being would mean harming oneself.

The practice of self-control, or 'Brahmacharya', is another cornerstone in the Indic ethical framework. Beyond its often-understood connotation of celibacy, Brahmacharya emphasizes the conservation of energy, control over desires and focused pursuit of knowledge. Such a discipline ensures one does not get swayed by transient temptations, ensuring ethical clarity.

∞

We are often confronted with interesting situations at the workplace. When someone sends us a diary or a box of sweets, we may choose to accept it. In contrast, if someone sends us something that has a higher perceived value in our minds, we may refuse it. Acceptance or refusal is purely based on our understanding of ethics. Therefore, if someone accepts anything in excess of what we would have done, would it be right to pass judgement on what their acceptance threshold may be?

The litmus test, in my opinion, is whether we believe that the person giving us something expects to get something in return. If the answer is yes, then even a cup of coffee does not pass muster.

Yet, perspectives on ethics change all over the world and the matter of ethics is interpreted differently in different countries.

But there are no shades of grey in the matter of ethics. It is either black or white.

In the vast expanse of Indic scriptures, ethics emerges not merely as a set of rules but as a nuanced understanding of life. It acknowledges the complexities, challenges and shades of grey that humans encounter. Through the concept of dharma, it provides a compass to navigate these intricacies. By emphasizing selfless action, discipline, non-violence and a larger cosmic order, the scriptures offer a roadmap to ethical living.

The wisdom of the Indic scriptures serves as a testament to the timeless nature of ethical values. In today's fast-paced, complex world, where moral dilemmas challenge us at every juncture, revisiting these ancient tenets can provide clarity and guidance. They remind us that ethical living is not just about individual well-being but about ensuring the harmony and prosperity of the entire cosmos.

MANAGEMENT MANTRAS

Ethics is concerned with determining the right and wrong actions of individuals, and its principles can be applied to various aspects of life, including business and management. In the context of management, ethics refers to the moral principles and values that govern the decision-making and behaviour of leaders and their organizations.

The meaning of ethics for managers is multifaceted, encompassing a range of responsibilities and obligations to stakeholders. For example, ethical managers are responsible for ensuring that their organizations conduct business in a way that is fair and equitable to all parties, including employees, customers, suppliers, shareholders and the community. This requires managers to act with integrity, honesty and fairness in all their dealings, as well as to ensure that their organizations adhere to relevant laws, regulations and ethical standards.

In addition to this, ethical managers also have an obligation to promote the well-being of their employees, including their safety, health and development. This means creating a work environment that is safe, healthy and supportive, providing fair compensation and benefits and investing in the development of their employees.

Furthermore, ethical managers also have a responsibility to promote environmental sustainability, ensuring that their organizations operate in a way that is environmentally responsible and sustainable over the long term. This involves reducing waste, conserving resources and minimizing the impact of their operations on the environment.

In conclusion, ethics is an essential aspect of effective

management, providing the framework and principles that guide decision-making and behaviour in organizations. Ethical managers are responsible for promoting the well-being of their employees and stakeholders, conducting business in a fair and equitable manner and operating in an environmentally sustainable manner. By embracing ethical principles and values, managers can create organizations that are not only successful but also responsible and respected.

TRUST

यो यो यां यां तनुं भक्त: श्रद्धयार्चितुमिच्छति।
तस्य तस्याचलां श्रद्धां तामेव विदधाम्यहम्।।

In whichever God a devotee places his trust,
God too steadies the trust of the devotee in that form.

—*Bhagavad Gita, Chapter 7, Verse 21*

The *Bhagavad Gita* emphasizes the importance of trust in the spiritual journey. In the *Gita*, Krishna tells Arjuna that he must trust his abilities and have faith in the divine guidance of the Lord. He also advises Arjuna to have faith in himself and use his own wisdom and intelligence to make decisions. This trust in oneself is essential for spiritual growth, as it allows one to make decisions based on their own understanding of the situation rather than relying solely on the advice of others.

Trust is an integral aspect of human relationships and

is the foundation of all successful personal and professional interactions. Trust is defined as the belief in the reliability, truth, ability or strength of someone or something. It is a complex emotional, psychological and behavioural phenomenon that plays a crucial role in shaping our perceptions, experiences and interactions.

Trust is built over time through experiences of consistent and reliable behaviour. It is important in both personal and professional relationships, and it is a key factor in determining the success of any collaboration or partnership. In personal relationships, trust is essential for the development of strong bonds between individuals, and it allows for open and honest communication. Trust in a romantic relationship, for example, leads to greater intimacy, commitment and satisfaction.

Trust is equally important in professional settings. It is a crucial component of team dynamics and can lead to improved cooperation, collaboration and productivity. Trust between employees and their employers can create a positive workplace culture and foster a sense of loyalty and commitment. Trust is also important for effective leadership, as leaders who are trusted are better able to motivate and inspire their teams.

However, trust can easily be broken and is difficult to rebuild once it has been damaged. Dishonest behaviour, lack of accountability and broken promises are just some of the ways in which trust can be eroded. Moreover, trust can also be impacted by larger societal issues such as corruption, deceit and greed, leading to a general sense of distrust in institutions and individuals.

Trust is an essential element of any successful relationship, whether it is between individuals,

communities or nations. In the Indic scriptures, trust is seen as a fundamental part of the spiritual path and is essential for achieving *moksha* or liberation from the cycle of rebirth.

The Vedas, the oldest scriptures of India, emphasize the importance of *rit*—the cosmic order, which is underpinned by trustworthiness and fidelity to the principles of righteousness. It ensures that the sun rises, the seasons change and all the cosmic events happen in order. On the human level, it implies that people should be trustworthy in their interactions.

The Upanishads discuss the importance of trusting the divine power of Brahman, the ultimate reality. The Upanishads also discuss the importance of trusting the teachings of the Vedas and encourage us to trust our inner wisdom and have faith in the guidance of the Vedas, rather than relying solely on any external authority. The Upanishads further delve into the concept of the *Atman* (soul) and *Brahman* (universal soul). Trust, in this context, evolves to an internal level, where one must trust the journey of the soul, understanding the impermanence of life and the ultimate convergence with the universe. It establishes a deep-seated faith in the cosmic order and the idea that everything happens for a reason.

In the *Ramayana*, Lord Rama is faced with difficult choices and he must trust his inner strength. His trust in the divine power of the Lord helps him to make the right decisions and to achieve his goals.

The *Bhagavad Gita*, Upanishads, *Ramayana* and *Mahabharata* all emphasize the importance of trust in the spiritual journey. Trust in oneself, the divine power of the Lord and the teachings of the Vedas is essential for spiritual growth.

In Buddhism, trust (often referred to as 'faith', or *shraddha* in Sanskrit) is not mere blind belief but a cultivated confidence in the teachings of the Buddha (the dharma) and the path of practice. It is trust in the four noble truths—the truths of suffering, its cause, its cessation and the path leading to its cessation. This trust encourages the practitioner to embark on the eightfold path, leading towards enlightenment.

Trust in Buddhism is also intimately connected with the practice of mindfulness and meditation. As one delves into the intricacies of their own mind, they begin to trust their innate potential for Buddhahood, the seed of enlightenment present in every sentient being. This inner trust facilitates spiritual growth and allows one to navigate the vicissitudes of life with equanimity.

In Sikhism, trust manifests as unwavering faith in the Divine (Waheguru) and acceptance of His Will (Hukam). The *Guru Granth Sahib*, the central religious scripture of Sikhism, echoes this sentiment in various hymns, emphasizing surrender and devotion. For Sikhs, trusting in the Divine Will means recognizing the transient nature of life and accepting both joy and sorrow with grace. Moreover, trust in Sikhism extends to the community or the *sangat*. Sikhs are encouraged to trust and support one another, uniting in their pursuit of spiritual growth and service to humanity. The principles of selfless service (seva) and community meals (langar) are testament to this collective trust, fostering unity and compassion.

Jainism, with its profound emphasis on non-violence (ahimsa), speaks of trust in a unique manner. At the core of ahimsa is recognition and respect for all living beings. This respect is based on a deep-seated trust in the intrinsic worth and sanctity of all forms of life. To harm another, in thought, word or deed, is a violation of this trust. Furthermore, Jainism introduces the concept of *anekantavada,* or the many-sidedness of truth. This philosophy teaches that truth has multiple facets, and one should be cautious in asserting a singular perspective. Inherent in this teaching is a trust in the diversity of viewpoints and a respect for the multiplicity of experiences.

MANAGEMENT MANTRAS

Trust is the foundation of any strong business, family or friendship. As Chanakya said, 'Trust is the foundation of any relationship.' Without trust, relationships can easily become strained or broken. We must work to build trust in our relationships and to maintain it.

Trust is a critical component in any organizational relationship and its importance for managers cannot be overstated. Trust is the foundation upon which all successful relationships are built and its presence can make the difference between success and failure. A lack of trust can create an environment of distrust, where employees are more likely to be disengaged and less likely to feel motivated to contribute to the success of the organization. In contrast, a high level of trust can help to create a positive work environment, where employees are motivated to contribute their best, and the manager is able to effectively lead the team to success.

The meaning of trust is twofold. First, trust involves the belief that the person being trusted is trustworthy and will act in a manner that is consistent with the expectations of the person who is placing their trust in them. For example, an employee trusts their manager to be fair and honest and to have their best interests at heart. Secondly, trust involves the willingness of the person placing the trust to take a risk and to believe in the person being trusted. This means that the employee is willing to believe in their manager even when there is no proof that they are trustworthy.

For managers, trust is essential to build strong relationships with employees. When employees trust their manager, they are more likely to be engaged and motivated to work hard and contribute to the success of the organization. Trust also fosters open and honest communication, which can help in reducing conflicts and improve collaboration. When employees feel that they can share their opinions and ideas freely with their manager, they are more likely to feel valued and respected. This, in turn, can lead to increased motivation and a greater commitment to the organization.

Trust is also critical to the success of the organization as a whole. A high level of trust between managers and employees can lead to improved performance and better outcomes. For example, employees who trust their manager are more likely to follow their guidance and work together to achieve common goals. This can lead to improved efficiency and productivity, and a more positive organizational culture.

In conclusion, trust is a critical component of any successful relationship and its meaning for managers is profound. Trust helps to build strong relationships with employees, fosters open and honest communication and is essential to the success of the organization.

VISHUDDHI CHAKRA

Connecting the Dots with Stakeholders

The fifth is the Vishuddhi or the Throat Chakra, associated with communication, self-expression and the ability to speak one's truth. When balanced, it promotes effective communication and encourages individuals to speak and live in alignment with their values. Ignorance refers to a lack of knowledge or understanding about a particular subject. In the context of stakeholders, ignorance can lead to a failure to understand the needs and concerns of stakeholders, resulting in a breakdown in communication and a lack of trust between the different parties.

Intuition refers to the ability to understand something instinctively, without the need for conscious reasoning. In the context of stakeholders, intuition can play a valuable role in helping leaders to understand the needs and concerns of their stakeholders.

Work culture is also a key consideration when it comes to stakeholders. The scriptures emphasize the importance of creating a positive work culture that supports all stakeholders. This can include creating a culture of respect, trust and open communication.

Empathy refers to the ability to understand and share the feelings of others. Hindu scriptures provide valuable insights into the role of stakeholders. By being aware of the potential pitfalls of ignorance and by being attuned to the subtle signals of intuition, leaders can build strong relationships with their stakeholders. Additionally, by creating a positive work culture and by being empathetic towards their stakeholders, leaders can foster a sense of shared purpose and commitment that benefits all parties involved.

IGNORANCE (AVIDYA/AGYAN)

अध्यात्मज्ञाननित्यत्वं तत्वज्ञानार्थदर्शनम्।
एतज्ज्ञानमिति प्रोक्तमज्ञानं यदतोऽन्यथा।।

Steadfastness in the knowledge of the Supreme Spirit,
and the perception of the omnipresent God as
the object of true knowledge is called knowledge;
what is contrary to this is ignorance.

—*Bhagavad Gita, Chapter 13, Verse 12*

In *Mahabharata*, at the end of the war when the Pandavas had won, Lord Krishna (as the charioteer) and Arjuna were still on their chariot, which also had a flag with Lord Hanuman on it. As was the tradition, the charioteer was expected to disembark first and stand at the foot of the chariot, waiting for the warrior to disembark. Arjuna, therefore, kept waiting for Lord Krishna to disembark.

When this did not happen, Arjuna got off from the carriage wondering why he had not been accorded this honour by Lord Krishna, given that he, Arjuna, had won the war for the Pandavas.

Immediately after Arjuna disembarked, Lord Krishna got off the chariot. The moment he disembarked, Lord Hanuman, who was sitting on the flag of the chariot, flew away. The moment Lord Hanuman flew away, the chariot exploded into a ball of fire and destroyed itself.

Lord Krishna went on to explain that Lord Hanuman was protecting the chariot during the war from all the powerful weapons thrown at it by the opposition. Lord Hanuman stayed on because he was serving Lord Krishna. He would not leave until Lord Krishna left. Had Lord Krishna stepped off the chariot before Arjuna left, Hanuman would have flown away, and Arjuna would have gone down in flames with the chariot. Lord Krishna's presence was the reason why the chariot held together after Arjuna disembarked.

Arjuna's arrogance at having won the war and feeling that he must be honoured as a great warrior blinded him to the fact that none of it would have been possible without the divine presence of Lord Krishna.

There is a difference between ignorance and stupidity. 'Ignorant' and 'stupid' are adjectives. Ignorant means lacking knowledge, while stupid means lacking brainpower. Both words can be derogatory if not used in the right context because our objective must not be to knowingly insult anyone.

For this chapter, we will focus only on ignorance and how the Hindu scriptures have handled this complex subject. The important lesson for us to remember is that being ignorant is nothing to be worried about.

Ignorance or *agyan*/*avidya* (avidya means to not know, perceive or understand) is either a lack of the right knowledge or a lack of the right interpretation of the facts available. This situation can easily be corrected.

Gyan or *vidya* is normally understood as knowledge and agyan or avidya is normally understood as ignorance.

Avidya in the earliest Vedic texts refers to ignorance. In later Vedic texts avidya evolves to include anything that is a 'positive hindrance' to spiritual or nonspiritual knowledge. In the Upanishads, the concept includes 'lack of knowledge, inadequate knowledge and false knowledge'.

In most matters where there is an opposite available, there are justifiable interpretations and perspectives for both ignorance and knowledge. This is true not only in Hinduism but also in other religions. Therefore, knowledge and ignorance are both relative terms.

The distinction between knowledge and ignorance is blurred when we cannot clearly determine what constitutes right or wrong knowledge. Most truths about the reality around us or our existence are relative and contextual and true only in a limited sense. This makes it even more difficult to distinguish knowledge from ignorance.

Ignorance can also be considered as a form of knowledge. Ignorance is a state of awareness or consciousness. We may know something that may not be right, especially when there is no unanimity about what constitutes true knowledge or when there are multiple perspectives on the same subject.

Ignorance, therefore, can also be understood as the lack of 'right' knowledge. We may know something but not in its entirety. We may have the right knowledge but may have drawn the wrong conclusion due to faulty reasoning or external influence. These situations and our perceptions about them can also be summed up as follows:

- I know.
- I don't know.
- I know and simultaneously I don't know.
- I neither know nor want to know.
- I know that I know.
- I know that I do not know.
- I know that I know but I also know that I don't know.
- I neither know that I know nor I know that I don't know.

The last two statements are a bit of a tongue twister but if we read them slowly and with comprehension, we will understand the meaning of each statement.

If we bring in another person into the same set of statements on our comprehension of knowledge, we can develop some additional set of statements, each carrying a different meaning, as follows:

- I know.
- You know.
- I do not know.
- You do not know.
- I know and simultaneously do not know.
- You know and you simultaneously do not know.
- I neither know nor want to know.
- You neither know nor want to know.
- I know that I know.
- You know that you know

- I know that you know.
- You know that I know.

The important point to remember is that no one may possess the 'absolute truth'. Everything we speak about has a 'context' attached to it. Our knowledge is mixed. Therefore, we cannot always determine with certainty what constitutes right or wrong knowledge or ignorance.

The story of the blind men and the elephant beautifully illustrates the meaning of ignorance or avidya/agyan. This story has its origins in ancient India and has been retold many times across the world.

It is the story of a group of blind men who have never come across an elephant before and who learn and imagine what the elephant might be by touching it. Each blind man feels a different part of the elephant's body, but only one part, such as the side or the tusk. They then describe the elephant based on their limited experience and their descriptions of the elephant are understandably different from each other. In some versions of the story, they suspect that the other person is dishonest, and they come to blows.

John Godfrey Saxe I, an American poet from the nineteenth century, is known for his retelling of the Indian parable of six blind men and the elephant.[*]

---

[*]Saxe, John Godfrey, *The Poems of John Godfrey Saxe*, J. Osgood, Boston, 1872, 259-261, https://archive.org/details/poemsofjohngodfr00saxeiala/page/258/mode/2up.

THE BLIND MEN AND THE ELEPHANT
A HINDOO FABLE

I.

It was six men of Indostan
To learning much inclined,
Who went to see the Elephant
(Though all of them were blind),
That each by observation
Might satisfy his mind.

II.

The *First* approached the Elephant,
And happening to fall
Against his broad and sturdy side,
At once began to bawl:
"God bless me!—but the Elephant
Is very like a wall!"

III.

The *Second*, feeling of the tusk,
Cried: "Ho!—what have we here
So very round and smooth and sharp?
To me 't is mighty clear
This wonder of an Elephant
Is very like a spear!"

IV.

The *Third* approached the animal,
And happening to take
The squirming trunk within his hands,
Thus boldly up and spake:

"I see," quoth he, "the Elephant
Is very like a snake!"

V.

The *Fourth* reached out his eager hand,
And felt about the knee.
"What most this wondrous beast is like
Is mighty plain," quoth he;
"'T is clear enough the Elephant
Is very like a tree!"

VI.

The *Fifth*, who chanced to touch the ear,
Said: "E'en the blindest man
Can tell what this resembles most;
Deny the fact who can,
This marvel of an Elephant
Is very like a fan!"

VII.

The *Sixth* no sooner had begun
About the beast to grope,
Than, seizing on the swinging tail
That fell within his scope,
"I see," quoth he, "the Elephant
Is very like a rope!"

VIII.

And so these men of Indostan
Disputed loud and long,
Each in his own opinion

> Exceeding stiff and strong,
> Though each was partly in the right,
> And all were in the wrong!
>
> MORAL.
> So, oft in theologic wars
> The disputants, I ween,
> Rail on in utter ignorance
> Of what each other mean,
> *And prate about an Elephant,*
> *Not one of them has seen!*

The moral of the story of the blind men and the elephant is that we humans tend to claim absolute truth based on our limited, subjective experiences, ignoring other people's limited, subjective experiences that may be equally true.

∞

Osho was a mystic, guru and spiritual teacher. One of the central themes that pervaded his vast body of work was the nature of ignorance and the path to enlightenment. He frequently spoke about ignorance as a veil or filter that distorts our perception of reality. Ignorance, in his view, is not just a lack of knowledge but rather a state of unconsciousness where one is detached from the present moment. He believed that our conditioning, societal norms and past experiences create layers of misconceptions and false beliefs that obscure the true nature of existence.

Osho viewed ignorance (avidya) as a primary source of human suffering. He said that our attachments, desires and ego arise from a state of unawareness, leading to endless cycles of pain, disappointment and unfulfillment. By remaining ignorant of our true nature, we become slaves to our fears, ambitions and illusions.

While he respected the role of intellectual knowledge, he made a distinction between knowledge and wisdom. Knowledge, he believed, was an accumulation of facts, while wisdom emerged from a deep understanding and awareness of life. He often stated that one could be highly educated and yet utterly ignorant in the spiritual sense. True wisdom, according to Osho, lay in transcending the intellectual mind and accessing the intuitive, more profound layers of consciousness.

His teachings offer a roadmap out of ignorance. Meditation, mindfulness and awareness were central to his approach. By practising meditation, one could peel away the layers of conditioning and enter a state of pure consciousness, free from the distractions and distortions of the mind. He emphasized the importance of living in the present moment, stating that the present is the only reality and the gateway to enlightenment. By moving beyond the mind and its constant chatter, one could experience life in its fullness and beauty.

Osho's thoughts on ignorance delve deep into the human psyche, unearthing the root causes of our suffering and offering a path to liberation. His teachings challenge us to question our beliefs, to shed our conditionings and to awaken to the timeless beauty of the present moment. In a world that often values information over insight, Osho's wisdom serves as a poignant reminder of the transformative power of self-awareness and the limitless potential that lies within each of us.

KNOWLEDGE CAN ALSO BE IGNORANCE

Whether you call it knowledge or ignorance, ignorance of self-knowledge, which constitutes spiritual ignorance, not only leads to suffering and spiritual downfall but also keeps you bound to the mortal world.

This type of ignorance is common to all living beings who are caught in the cycle of births and deaths. Such people then mistake truth for falsehood and unreal for real and engage in actions spurred by their desires that lead to their suffering and rebirth.

The era of smartphones, spearheaded by Apple, brought in an era of easy access to knowledge, and Google ensured that information was available at our fingertips. Social media platforms further democratize information.

In the Information Age, ignorance is no longer an excuse.

Chanakya said, 'Knowledge is lost without putting it into practice; a man is lost due to ignorance; an army is lost without a commander.'

What we know influences us. What we don't know influences us even more. Ignorance is not only about knowing something but also about an unwillingness to learn. It is not only about what we do not know but also what we refuse to learn and accept.

The root of the word ignorance is 'ignore'. It is defined as a situation where a person is willingly refusing knowledge. We need to have an open mind, and understanding and accepting another person's perspective and reality can be a cause for fear and uncertainty. This reflects our fear of growing further.

Not knowing the truth does not make us ignorant but

not wanting to know the truth does. There is no better way to fight ignorance than with knowledge. Following are some thoughts on how we can handle ignorance:

1. Start with ourselves: We need to develop a growth mindset of learning every day. An inquisitive mind will help us to keep asking questions in our quest for knowledge.
2. Keep an open mind: Understanding and accepting that we may not have all the answers is half the battle won. Sometimes we consciously make bad choices but with an open mind, we can find ways to overcome these mistakes.
3. Avoid judging or criticizing: Not judging someone or criticizing someone is the first step to overcoming our ignorance. Appreciating and accepting that others have a point of view that could be different from ours is important. We can certainly offer our opinion, but recognizing that the other person may not agree with us.
4. Do not expect others to accept your point of view: If our point of view is logically stated, the other person may align their views with ours. Ignorant people may not listen to us, which must not affect us.
5. Surround ourselves with open-minded people: This is one way to encourage dialogue and to understand multiple perspectives on any matter. Once we have the information, we can draw our conclusions. Once again, our conclusions may not necessarily be accepted by others.
6. Do not use ignorance as an excuse: Ignorance is not an excuse. It is a choice. We choose ignorance every time we

refuse knowledge or an improvement in ourselves. The choices we make have an impact on our current reality.
7. Seek multiple inputs to gain knowledge: In our digital world, we tend to form opinions based on social media, which is a dangerous trend. A lot is stated on social media that could be biased or could be an agenda of the person who puts out said information. It is, therefore, incumbent upon us to check the facts and then form our opinions rather than simply accept whatever we may have read.

   In our quest for knowledge, we need to explore as many databases as possible. One source is not enough. We need to recheck and reconfirm the information based upon which we will form our opinion.
8. Ignorance is bliss: This is a fallacy that has been passed down the ages and we have accepted this without questioning it. If we were to accept ignorance being blissful as a paradigm, imagine what this could do to our society.

   We must recognize and accept that ignorance is not bliss.

MANAGEMENT MANTRAS

Ignorance, or lack of knowledge or information, can have significant consequences for managers and their ability to effectively lead and make decisions. In today's rapidly changing business environment, it is more important than ever for managers to continuously seek out and acquire new information and insights to stay ahead of the curve and stay relevant in their roles.

One of the main challenges posed by ignorance for managers is the potential for decision-making biases and errors. When managers are not well-informed about a particular issue or decision, they may rely on incorrect assumptions, stereotypes or past experiences, leading to poor decisions. For example, a manager who is unfamiliar with a new technology may make a decision based on outdated information, causing the company to miss out on potential opportunities or face difficulties implementing a new strategy.

Ignorance can also lead to missed opportunities, particularly in a rapidly changing business landscape. Managers who are not up-to-date on the latest developments in their industry or market may miss out on valuable opportunities to expand their business, invest in new technologies or form partnerships with other companies. Furthermore, managers who are unaware of changes in the competitive landscape may find themselves at a disadvantage with competitors who are better informed and better positioned to succeed.

Another challenge posed by ignorance is the potential for miscommunication and misunderstandings. Managers who are not fully informed about a particular issue or decision may misinterpret information or give incorrect instructions to their employees, leading to confusion, frustration and decreased efficiency. This can also harm relationships with stakeholders, such as customers, partners or suppliers, and damage the company's reputation.

To address the challenges posed by ignorance, managers must take proactive steps to continuously acquire new information and stay up-to-date on industry developments. This can include reading industry publications and attending conferences, networking with peers and experts and seeking out opportunities for professional development. In addition, managers should seek out diverse perspectives and be open to feedback from their employees and other stakeholders, as this can provide valuable insights and help managers stay informed about changes in the market or industry.

Therefore, ignorance can have significant consequences for managers, from decision-making errors to missed opportunities and miscommunication. However, by proactively seeking out new information and staying up-to-date on industry developments, managers can mitigate the risks posed by ignorance and position themselves for success in today's rapidly changing business landscape.

INTUITION

तेषां सततयुक्तानां भजतां प्रीतिपूर्वकम्।
ददामि बुद्धियोगं तं येन मामुपयान्ति ते।।
तेषामेवानुकम्पार्थमहमज्ञानजं तमः।
नाशयाम्यात्मभावस्थो ज्ञानदीपेन भास्वता।।

To those who are constantly engaged in devotion with love,
I will provide the divine knowledge
with which they can attain Me.
Because of the compassion I have for them,
I will destroy the darkness born of ignorance
that dwells within their hearts
with the shining lamp of knowledge.

—*Bhagavad Gita, Chapter 10, Verses 10–11*

Paramhansa Yogananda* said that in the life of every person, two forces of knowledge are operative from birth:

1. the power of human reason, along with its satellites of sensation, perception, conception and so forth;
2. the power of intuition.

Intuition is a higher level of knowledge that enables human beings to experience the presence of the Supreme *Brahman* within.

The role of 'intuition' or inner knowing emerges as an integral aspect of one's spiritual journey in our scriptures. Intuition is not merely a hunch or a gut feeling. It is a profound, direct experience of truth. While the intellect relies on external data, intuition taps into an inner reservoir of wisdom.

Traditional systems of Indian philosophy speak of different means of acquiring knowledge. One such means is *pratyaksha* or direct perception. While on the surface, pratyaksha refers to knowledge gained through the senses, certain philosophical interpretations also classify intuitive knowledge, where one perceives truths beyond sensory perception, as a form of pratyaksha. Intuition, in this sense, is a direct experience of the truth, without the intervention of rational or logical processes.

The Upanishads frequently speak of a higher knowledge that transcends the intellect. Passages describe sages and

---

*Yogananda, Paramahansa, 'Beyond Thought and Intellect: The Unlimited Insight of Soul Intuition', *Yogoda Satsanga Society of India*, https://yssofindia.org/spiritual/Beyond-Thought-and-Intellect-The-Unlimited-Insight-of-Soul-Intuition.

seekers who, after much contemplation and meditation, gain insights not through logical analysis but through a sudden flash of understanding, an intuitive realization. This is often referred to as the knowledge of the 'Self' or 'Atman', which we have discussed earlier in this book. It is an understanding that is beyond words and intellectual constructs.

Lord Krishna emphasizes the importance of 'Buddhi', a term that signifies both intellect and intuition. While the intellect divides, analyses and categorizes, intuition perceives, synthesises and grasps the essence. The *Gita* suggests that true wisdom arises when one can harmoniously integrate both intellect and intuition in their actions and decisions.

In many Indic traditions, the Guru or spiritual teacher holds a significant place. While scriptures provide knowledge, the Guru offers direct experience. The relationship between the disciple and the Guru is not merely academic; it is deeply intuitive. The Guru, through their grace, can ignite the intuitive spark within the disciple, allowing them to perceive truths that were previously hidden.

This knowledge cannot be handed down or taught; it is an insight that each of us has to experience on our own. Our understanding and experience of the learnings from our scriptures are partly through reading the written texts and partly through an intuitive understanding that is gained from our families and the community we live in, through stories and experiences, through festivals and the environment around us in most of our homes.

Intuition is a heightened, refined sense in addition to our five senses.

Intuition is not easily recognized because it is not easy to sense, other than when we are in touch with who we are on the inside. That is why it is more complex than any other emotion. Some people confuse it with instinct. However, intuition and instinct are completely different.

Instinct is the first biological and psychological thought and reaction that comes to our mind when we are faced with an uncertain situation. It is a raw emotion and some instincts do not necessarily serve our purpose in the modern world.

In contrast, intuition is a signal that we get, indicating whether something is right for us or not, based on very little information that we may have at that moment. Therefore, we cannot explain intuition with perfect reasoning. Intuition is felt or experienced by us at a deeper level.

Intuition has to do with our connection with the world around us. It is more refined and not raw like an instinct. It gives biological or physical signals based on which we decide if something is good or not for us. Intuition is often referred to as 'gut feeling', the way we feel within during some situations.

Instinct is a common trait in every human and animal. But a strong intuition is like a gift. Not everyone possesses it.

Based on our intuitive capabilities, we may be able to sense or know about things even before we have more information about the situation. It takes immense self-conviction to believe in one's intuition. Our intuition may or may not be true but it certainly enables us to prepare ourselves mentally to expect any situation that may be presented before us.

From a management perspective, an intuitive decision-making capability is also referred to as our 'sixth sense' or 'gut feeling or 'inner knowing'. Our sixth sense gives us the ability to gather information that other individuals may miss. It is the opposite of rational decision-making in which individuals use analytics, facts and a step-by-step process to reach a decision.

Understanding our intuitive capabilities can be a big asset for us. Trusting our intuition is even more important. We are often faced with a situation where our intuition tells us to handle the situation differently from the options presented before us; which option we select or whether we go with our intuition is something we face so many times, possibly every day.

Let us discuss some advantages of understanding our intuition:

1. *Intuition keeps us aligned*: Deep down within us, we know when something is not working out. Our rational mind could be telling us to go ahead with a transaction while our gut feeling might be telling us to run. It is often better to follow the gut feeling. There will be greater satisfaction within us. Of course, the gut feeling could be wrong but at least we will be prepared to handle it since it was our own decision.

2. *Our response time improves*: Studies have shown that intuition speeds up our response time. The same study found that 'nonconscious emotional information can boost accuracy and confidence.'[*] Leading with intuition could make us quicker and more accurate. Of course, intuition must be backed by hard evidence of data and facts.

---

[*]Lufityanto, Galang, Chris Donkin, and Joel Pearson, 'Measuring Intuition: Nonconscious Emotional Information Boosts Decision Accuracy and Confidence', *Psychological Science*, Vol. 27, No. 5, 2016, 622–634. https://doi.org/10.1177/0956797616629403.

3. *Intuition can make us more customer-centric*: We get a lot of data about our customers through research. But we need to connect with the customers at a deeper level to understand their needs, expectations and complaints, if any. Intuition brings us closer to natural intelligence and the flow of the universe. In doing so, we can gain access to information that seems to appear from nowhere. It's just a deep sense of knowing. Listen to your gut when it tells you what people want. It knows more than you think.
4. *Intuition can make us a better leader*: When we go with our gut feeling, our decision-making can become a lot clearer. We will be able to stop 'second-guessing' and give better directions to our teams. With greater clarity in our minds, we will be able to stay true to our vision.

Intuition coupled with data is the perfect combination. When I get a feeling that something will resonate, I generally run with it. And when we practise that skill over and over, the intuitive muscle gets stronger.

Intuition is a powerful tool that's available to us all; why not step out of our comfort zones and start using it?

FIVE FORMS OF INTUITION

Intuition can express itself in any of the below five forms[*]:

1. *Basic feeling*: Every human being has this. An intuition for self-preservation exists in all living beings. This form

---

[*]Sri Daya Mata, *Finding the Joy Within You*, Yogoda Satsanga Society of India/Self-Realization Fellowship, Kolkata, 1 April 2021, http://yogananda.com.au/dayamata/daya_mata_intuition.html.

of intuition exists even in our sleep and comes from our unconscious mind.

2. *Knowledge of life forces*: This form of intuition could lead us to sense subtle sounds, lights, sensations and fragrances of flavours. These are not outward sensations; they have nothing to do with the physical sense organs.
3. *Knowledge of the mind*: When we reach a stage where we have an understanding of our mind, we are not conscious of the outside world. It is possible for us to see a vision of what may happen.
4. *Knowledge of intellect*: This is when we are able to discern what is happening and could also be referred to as wisdom.
5. *Knowledge of bliss*: This is a highly evolved form of intuition and is possibly found in religious leaders who have been able to connect with their souls.

The first form of intuition exists within everyone. The next four forms of intuition need to be developed by training our minds.

ARTIFICIAL INTELLIGENCE, ARTIFICIAL INTUITION AND INTUITION

New technologies such as artificial intelligence (AI), machine learning and natural language processing are emerging fast. These are empowering business leaders to make better, more informed and effective decisions. Despite these advancements, many executives remain comfortable with their traditional decision-making methods, often choosing to go with their gut feeling over data analytics. In fact, according to a Forbes/PwC survey, two-thirds of business leaders acknowledge that their own company's decision-making is only somewhat or rarely data-driven.*

But should leaders trust their instinct or embrace data-driven decision-making?

Many top executives cite intuition as the reason for their success, with leadership often being associated with decisiveness and quick thinking. Seasoned leaders are not only confident in their instincts but also adept at making others feel confident in their judgement. Going with our gut can help us make faster, more accurate decisions, as human decision-making are based on more than just instinct. We make choices based on other factors such as our experiences, values and empathy.

Intuition is a state of mind that enables the capacity to perceive, interpret and operationalize information from an ordinary level to an in-depth analysis of inputs. This is what we know as logical thinking, enabling high-level function for the brain.

For years, imitating human intuition has seemed impossible. It was believed that the highest level for AI is predictive analysis to forecast the future based on input data.

To be a great leader in this age, executives must strike a delicate balance between human and machine thinking. Becoming truly data-driven will require organizations to have the leadership strength and talent to leverage the right information at the right time and act.

---

*PwC and Forbes Insights, 'Data-driven: Big Decisions in the Intelligence Age', *PwC Big Decisions Report*, PwC, 19 July 2016, https://images.forbes.com/forbesinsights/StudyPDFs/PwC-Big_Decisions-REPORT.pdf.

Of course, human judgment is at the centre of all successful data analysis.

Artificial intuition is the next step for AI, and it can revolutionize the machine-learning process. From the discovery of fire by our ancestors to the current era when traveling to other planets isn't out of reach, human intuition has evolved dramatically, with a capacity to grow over its limitations. But can artificial intuition mimic human intuition?

Artificial intuition still has a long road ahead to be operationalized and find its place in the market. While almost all industries can potentially benefit from it, some may have a better opportunity to exploit its capabilities. It is a matter of time before artificial intuition will be at the core of any business operation in big companies.

MANAGEMENT MANTRAS

Intuition is a critical component of effective decision-making for managers. Despite the increasing reliance on data-driven decision-making and artificial intelligence tools, intuition remains a valuable tool in today's rapidly changing and complex business environment.

Intuition can be defined as the unconscious processing of information and experiences, leading to an immediate sense or gut feeling about a situation. It is often considered the result of years of experience and exposure to different scenarios, allowing managers to quickly process information and identify patterns that may not be immediately obvious to others. This ability to process information quickly and effectively can be especially valuable in high-pressure situations where time is limited and the consequences of a decision are significant.

In addition to its speed, intuition also allows managers to take a more holistic approach to decision-making. By relying on their instincts and experience, managers can consider all aspects of a situation, including human emotions and motivations, rather than just relying on hard data. This broader perspective can result in more creative and innovative solutions to complex business challenges.

Another important aspect of intuition is its ability to help managers navigate uncertainty and ambiguity. In many cases, there may be limited data or conflicting information, making it difficult to make a decision based solely on facts. In these situations, intuition can serve as a valuable backup system, allowing managers to make informed decisions even in the absence of complete information.

Intuition remains a relevant and valuable tool for managers in today's fast-paced and complex business environment. However, intuition should not be relied on exclusively. Managers need to balance their instincts with data analysis and other forms of evidence-based decision-making. This helps to avoid biases and ensures that decisions are made with a complete understanding of the situation.

WORK CULTURE

इच्छन्ति देवा: सुन्वन्तं न स्वप्नाय स्पृहयन्ति।
यन्ति प्रमादमतन्द्रा:॥

The Devatas desire him who offers worship and works hard.
They do not like him who loves to sleep and is lazy.
The hard-working person gets great praise from them.

—*Rig Veda, Book 8, Chapter 2, Verse 18*

कर्मण्येवाधिकारस्ते मा फलेषु कदाचन।
मा कर्मफलहेतुर्भूर्मा ते सङ्गोऽस्त्वकर्मणि॥

—*Bhagavad Gita, Chapter 2, Verse 47*

This is a well-known and recognized verse from the *Bhagavad Gita*, signifying the importance of work in our lives. It states that we must always be ready to do our work and not care for the fruits of our actions. We should neither consider ourselves the cause of the results of the activities we perform nor be attached to inaction. When we understand the importance of our work and do it sincerely, we experience real satisfaction in our lives. It is necessary for us to understand the importance of doing our work.

Thus, the four aspects of work outlined in the *Gita* are:

1. We need to perform our duty and not be concerned with the results.
2. The fruits of our actions are not for our enjoyment.
3. While working, we should give up our ego, i.e. the pride of being the doer.
4. We should not be attached to inaction.

Our scriptures present a multifaceted and profound view of culture. They don't just offer a set of beliefs or practices but provide a comprehensive worldview that integrates the ethical, philosophical and cosmological dimensions of existence.

Culture, in the broadest sense, refers to the collective beliefs, practices, customs, arts and shared knowledge of a particular group of people.

The ancient sages of India encapsulated human aspirations into four primary goals, or *Purusharthas*. *Dharma* (duty and righteousness), *artha* (wealth and material prosperity), *kama* (desire and pleasure), and *moksha* (liberation). Culture is a harmonious pursuit of these four goals, ensuring that material aspirations do not override ethical and spiritual pursuits.

Culture, therefore, is the embodiment and manifestation of dharma in every aspect of human life.

One of the defining features of the Indic scriptures is their appreciation for diversity. This respect for diverse paths underscores the rich tapestry of Indic culture, where various traditions, practices and schools of thought coexist harmoniously. Our scriptures encourage living in harmony with nature and all living beings.

Indic culture celebrates life in its manifold expressions. The myriad festivals, rituals and ceremonies that have their roots in the scriptures honour various deities, seasons and life events, encapsulating a holistic view of existence. The underlying message is one of gratitude, reverence and joyous participation in the cosmic dance of existence.

Mahatma Gandhi has also said that work is worship. Life is sacred, and performing our duty is our dharma, which means 'way of righteousness, religion and fulfilment of duty'. From this view, every deed is a part of our religious practice. Everything we do is an act of worship and faith. Our worship in the temple is part of our dharma, and our work is equally a part of our dharma.

∞

Lord Krishna explains two types of work culture to Arjuna in Chapter 16 of the *Gita*.
1. *Daivi sampat* or divine work culture, which means the presence of fearlessness, purity, sense-control, sacrifice, straightforwardness, calmness, gentleness, modesty and absence of fault-finding, greed, envy and pride.
2. *Asuri sampat* or demonic work culture, which means the presence of egoism, delusion, improper performance or work that is not oriented towards service.

WHAT IS GREATER: KARMA OR BUDDHI?

Arjuna asks Lord Krishna in the *Gita*, 'Which is greater? Work (*karma*) or intellect (*buddhi*)?

The word *buddhi* is derived from the Sanskrit root '*budh*', which means 'to wake, be awake, observe, heed, attend, learn, become aware of, to know and be conscious again'.

The Vedas prescribe work according to our *varna* or our physical and mental make-up. The four varnas that have been discussed in this book are Brahmin, Kshatriya, Vaishya and Shudra.

It is important to understand that Lord Krishna says that the different *varna* are not to be determined by birth but by one's ability and capability.

In an ideal society, the state governs in accordance with the directions of the sages and priests. In modern society, the economy is critical and therefore the merchants have more importance.

Society can be compared to a body. The Brahmins (the intellectuals, philosophers, sages, priests and teachers) represent the head. The Kshatriyas (warriors, kings, politicians, military and police) are the arms. The Vaishyas (farmers, merchants and bankers) are the belly. The Shudras (skilled workers, artists, musicians, actors and everyone who serves others) are the legs.

The body is meant to be directed by the head. The function of the arms is to protect the body. The stomach's function is to nourish the body and distribute energy, and the function of the legs is to move the body.

BUILD A WORKPLACE CULTURE

Culture is the character and personality of your organization. It is what makes your business unique and is the sum of its values, traditions, beliefs, interactions, behaviours and attitudes.

A positive workplace culture attracts talent, drives engagement, impacts happiness and satisfaction and affects performance. The personality of your business is influenced by everything. Leadership, management, workplace practices, policies, people, etc., significantly impact culture.

The biggest mistake organizations make is letting their work culture form on its own without first defining what they want it to be.

Company culture is the social operating system that influences how your employees work with each other, the customers and the community. It has the potential to either help a company thrive or cause it to suffer. Leaders must be willing to explore many ideas to improve workplace culture. A positive company culture does not happen by itself—it takes planning and effort. The leaders need to lead by example.

Building culture cannot be delegated to the Chief Human Resources Officer.

Let us look at a few steps that leaders can take to improve and build workplace culture.

1. *Awaken the 'Lord Krishna' inside each leader*: Encourage leaders to become mentors and coaches for the employees. Leaders play a major role in shaping corporate work culture. Lord Krishna was possibly the first 'coach' in the world, not only for Arjuna but also for all the five Pandava brothers. The *Mahabharata* is replete with examples where He encouraged and guided them through their conflict with the Kauravas.

2. *Communicate clarity of purpose to each leader, like Chanakya did for Chandragupta Maurya*: Chanakya encouraged young Chandragupta Maurya to see the bigger picture of unifying various kingdoms into one country, Bharata. Connecting employees to a purpose is a powerful way to improve workplace culture. Without a sense of purpose, it's almost impossible to work towards making an impact, helping others or changing the world.

   Connecting both current and potential employees to your organization's purpose is a critical step to improving workplace culture.

3. *Recognize the work done by employees, like Lord Rama does throughout the* Ramayana: Acknowledging the work being done by people in one's organization motivates them to go beyond the call of duty. We see this repeatedly in the *Ramayana*. Lord Rama even acknowledged Ravana's wisdom when he lay defeated on the battlefield, and asked Lakshmana to go and seek knowledge from Ravana.

    Recognition also carries many other significant benefits. This includes attracting talent, retaining talent, increasing job performance and more innovation. It is a vital component of building or improving workplace culture. It is also important to ensure that peer-to-peer recognition is enabled and promoted, and not just leader-driven recognition.

We must remember that culture is always a work in progress. It can and will change. Leaders must ensure that culture is as important as their business strategy. It's too significant to ignore, and shaping it is one of your most important responsibilities as leaders and human resources professionals.

Peter Drucker is famously believed to have said, 'Culture eats strategy for breakfast.'

We need a strong culture to build a strong organization.

MANAGEMENT MANTRAS

Work culture refers to the beliefs, values, attitudes, behaviours and practices that characterize an organization. It encompasses the collective characteristics of an organization's employees, their interactions and their approach to work. Work culture is an essential aspect of an organization's success and can significantly impact the motivation, satisfaction and performance of employees.

For managers, work culture has a significant meaning as they play a crucial role in shaping and maintaining the organizational culture. As leaders, managers are responsible for creating an environment that fosters collaboration, innovation and employee satisfaction. A positive work culture can lead to improved employee morale, higher levels of productivity and a reduced rate of turnover. In contrast, a negative work culture can have the opposite effect—leading to low morale, decreased productivity and increased turnover.

Managers can use work culture to drive their organization's success by setting an example for their employees, which they can do by demonstrating the values and behaviours that are essential for the organization's success. For example, if the organization values teamwork, managers should encourage collaboration and motivate employees to work together. Similarly, if the organization values innovation, managers should provide opportunities for employees to be creative and take risks. By modelling the desired behaviours, managers can inspire their employees to adopt similar attitudes and practices.

In addition, work culture can provide a sense of identity and purpose for employees, which is essential for their motivation and job satisfaction. When employees feel that they are part of a team, they are more likely to be engaged and committed to the organization's goals. A positive work culture can also create a sense of belonging, which can lead to improved employee morale and a reduction in employee turnover.

Furthermore, work culture can impact employee performance by setting expectations for behaviour and performance. For example, if the work culture emphasizes a focus on results, employees are likely to be more productive and motivated to achieve their goals. In contrast, if the work culture is relaxed and informal, employees may not feel the need to work as hard or be as productive. Managers should use the work culture to set expectations for employee behaviour and performance and encourage employees to meet or exceed those expectations.

Managers play a critical role in shaping and maintaining the work culture, which can then be used to drive organizational success.

EMPATHY

अद्वेष्टा सर्वभूतानां मैत्र: करुण एव च॥
निर्ममो निरहङ्कार: समदु:खसुख: क्षमी॥

My true devotee does not feel hatred for any being,
but is friendly and compassionate towards all,
and is free from egoism.

—*Bhagavad Gita, Chapter 12, Verse 13*

In the *Bhagavad Gita*, Lord Krishna emphasizes that one should act selflessly and without desire, always putting others before the self. This philosophy is based on the belief that all souls are equal and that one should treat others with the same respect and love that one would want for themselves.

Our scriptures, such as the Vedas, *Bhagavad Gita* and Upanishads, discuss how all souls are connected and how one should treat others with kindness and understanding. The importance of empathy and compassion for all living beings is constantly emphasized.

Empathy, the ability to understand and share the feelings of another, is a universal human value found in various religious and spiritual traditions worldwide. An exploration of Hindu scriptures reveals profound teachings on empathy, suggesting that it is not only an emotional response but also a spiritual practice that leads one towards enlightenment.

At the heart of many teachings from our scriptures lies the principle of 'ahimsa' or non-violence. The concept goes beyond just refraining from physical violence. It is an invitation to cultivate a mindset that avoids harm in thought, word and deed. Implicit in this principle is a deep sense of empathy: for one to avoid causing harm, one must first understand the feelings and experiences of another.

The Upanishads refer to the interconnectedness of all beings. The famous declaration *tat tvam asi* (thou art that or you are one) in the *Chandogya Upanishad* is a testament to this interconnectedness. When one sees oneself in another, empathy becomes a natural outcome. Recognizing the divine essence in every being makes it easier to understand and feel their joy, pain and struggles.

In the *Gita* Lord Krishna advises Arjuna to rise above personal likes and dislikes and to see all beings with an equal eye. This equanimity, which is grounded in empathy, enables one to act with compassion and justice.

Empathy in our scriptures is not just presented as philosophical teachings but is also beautifully encapsulated in various stories and parables that emphasize the virtues of compassion, understanding and love. Characters like King Harishchandra, who endured immense personal suffering to uphold the truth, or Yashoda, who loved Lord Krishna selflessly, exemplify empathy in their actions.

Empathy, as viewed in Hindu scriptures, is more than just an emotional attribute. It is a deeply spiritual practice rooted in the philosophy of oneness and interconnectedness. By cultivating empathy, one not only creates harmony in the external world but also progresses on the path of self-realization and ultimate liberation.

∞

Empathy means that in our interactions with others, we should always put ourselves in their place and imagine how they would feel. When we do this, we realize that we have to be fair, just and kind towards others. Just as we do not like being attacked, beaten, lied to, cheated and so on, others also do not like it. Empathy helps us to understand the feelings and perspectives of others and stops us from behaving unjustly towards them.

An empathetic person makes sure that none of their actions hurt others. They are not only compassionate towards others but also share other's joys and sorrows.

Mahatma Gandhi once went on a tour of a village in India. He reached a hut in which lived a family comprising several individuals. Surprisingly, the individuals would come out only one at a time to see him. When the first individual went back in, the second came out. When the second went back in, the third came out. Gandhi was surprised at this behaviour of the family and asked the other villagers why they did not come all out at once to greet him. A villager replied, 'They are from a very poor family and have only one piece of cloth to cover the upper half of their bodies. Therefore, they are forced to share this piece of cloth and come out only one person at a time so that they are fully covered in front of you.'

Gandhi was distressed after hearing this. He thought that if his countrymen were that poor, he had no right to wear multiple clothes. From that day onwards, he decided that he would wear only one piece of cloth. The rich lawyer, who was fond of wearing expensive clothing, could then be seen only in a loincloth wherever he went.

EMPATHY, NON-VIOLENCE AND KARMA

The concept of non-violence (ahimsa) is closely related to empathy. This principle states that one should not cause harm to any living being and should instead strive to live in harmony with all creatures. This extends not only to physical violence but also to mental and emotional harm, emphasizing the importance of speaking and acting with kindness and compassion.

Empathy is also linked to karma, which states that every action has consequences and that one reaps what one sows. This means that one should act with empathy and kindness as it is the right thing to do and will lead to positive consequences in this and future lives.

Hindu scriptures also talk about the importance of putting oneself in the other person's shoes to understand their perspective. This is also referred to as collective vision and emphasizes the need to see the world from a holistic perspective and to understand how our actions impact others.

Empathy is an integral part of Hinduism and is emphasized in the scriptures as a way to nurture compassion, kindness and understanding towards all living beings.

By embracing empathy, one can lead a more fulfilling life and make the world a better place.

EMPATHY IN BUDDHISM

Buddha taught that the root of suffering is ignorance and that the key to ending suffering is to cultivate compassion and empathy for all beings. Empathy plays a crucial role in Buddhism because it helps practitioners to connect with others and view the world with compassion.

Buddha advocated the development of empathy through the practice of mindfulness, which involves being fully present in the moment and paying attention to one's thoughts, emotions and sensations. Through mindfulness, practitioners can learn to see things from different perspectives and cultivate a sense of interconnection with all beings. This helps them to develop compassion and feel empathy for others, even those they may not know or understand.

The well-known eightfold path in Buddhism stresses on empathy or a compassionate attitude towards others. It further includes developing the right views, speech, action, livelihood, effort, mindfulness and concentration. These help the practitioners to cultivate empathy and compassion, as well as overcome ignorance and suffering.

By developing empathy, we can connect with others and view the world with compassion, which is an essential step in the path to enlightenment. Through this understanding of empathy, Buddhism offers a path to a life of compassion, kindness and peace.

MANAGEMENT MANTRAS

Chanakya believed in the importance of empathy and emotional intelligence in leadership and decision-making. He wrote in the *Arthashastra* that a leader devoid of feelings and emotions cannot attain success.

He also emphasized the need to understand and connect with the emotions and experiences of others. He said, 'One should listen to the words of the obedient, consult the wise and follow the footsteps of the good.'

True empathy involves going beyond our thoughts and feelings to truly understand and identify with the feelings of others. The importance of self-awareness and introspection in developing empathy is critical as one must first understand themselves in order to understand others.

By developing empathy, we can break down the barriers of separation and judgment, leading to greater compassion and love for all beings.

AJNA CHAKRA

Holistic Communication and Awareness

The sixth is the Ajna or the Third-Eye Chakra, which is associated with intuitive listening and involves going beyond the literal words spoken to grasp the deeper meaning or intention behind them. When balanced, it supports clarity in mental reception and helps us receive information without distortion, confusion or misinterpretation, contributing to effective communication. Our Vedas and Upanishads emphasize the importance of communication based on a holistic approach to life, which involves mindfulness, gratitude, duty and active listening.

One of the key aspects of holistic communication and awareness is gratitude, which is considered an essential component of a holistic life. The *Bhagavad Gita* teaches that being grateful for what we have and accepting everything that comes our way with grace is a crucial part of leading a fulfilling life.

Duty, or dharma, refers to the moral and ethical obligations one holds in life. Rooted in ancient wisdom, it emphasizes righteous action and maintaining social and cosmic order. Dharma varies by one's age, caste, gender and occupation, guiding individuals towards righteous living and spiritual growth.

Career challenges are inevitable, but the way we approach them can have a significant impact on our communication and overall well-being. The law of *karma* teaches that everything we do has consequences and that our present circumstances are a result of our past actions.

Active listening involves being fully present and attentive to the person we are communicating with. By actively listening, we can become more aware of the needs and concerns of others, which can help us communicate more effectively and build stronger relationships.

Our scriptures provide a rich source of wisdom by emphasizing the importance of gratitude, duty and active listening in our communication, which subsequently helps in overcoming challenges in our careers.

GRATITUDE

नाकस्य पृष्ठे अधि तिष्ठति श्रितो य: पृणाति स ह देवेषु गच्छति।
तस्मा आपो घृतमर्षन्ति सिन्धवस्तस्मा इयं दक्षिणा पिन्वते सदा।।

Gratitude is the fairest blossom that springs from the soul.

—*Rig Veda, Book 1, Chapter 125, Verse 5*

When Lord Rama was banished to the forest, Bharata, his brother, came to see him with a large number of people, a couple of horses and wealth. Bharata wanted to join Lord

Rama in the jungle. Lord Rama asked Bharata to go back with everything he had brought except food for the horses who had brought Rama, Sita and Lakshmana to the edge of the forest. Lord Rama wanted to show his gratitude to the horses and tried to repay his debt to them with the food he took from Bharata.

Gratitude originates from the Latin word 'gratia' meaning grace or thankfulness. It is a value that is usually ingrained in us, a value that is given importance in every religion of the world.

In India, to express gratitude, we fold our hands, bow our heads and then say, *dhanyavada*, meaning 'thank you for helping me!' Hinduism teaches us to be humble. Gratitude, in Sanskrit, is *kritajnya*.

Karna's biological parents, Kunti and the Sun God, never claimed him as their son; his mother, Kunti, abandoned him at birth. He was brought up by a charioteer and was always looked down upon because he was not from a high-born family. Duryodhana, irrespective of his flaws, recognized Karna's skills as a top archer and made him the ruler of a few villages to accord him the stature he deserved. Karna, to show his gratitude, overlooked all his flaws and served Duryodhana till the very end, even after Lord Krishna and his mother disclosed about his birth parents.

A simple way to understand gratitude is to see how we look at life: half full or half empty? Yet, when something good or helpful is done, we tend to overlook it or simply treat it as something that we expected in the first place. No acknowledgement is shown and no gratitude is expressed.

But if we see a shortcoming, we are very quick to point it out!

Ravana was a knowledgeable person. He had prayed to Lord Shiva and was blessed with a boon that would make him invincible to all Gods. His gratitude evolved into a massive ego, which led him to take the steps that he did. He had asked for invincibility from all Gods but missed asking for the same from humans and animals. When his atrocities became too much for the people to bear, Lord Vishnu had to take birth as a human being (Lord Rama) and with an army of monkeys, he defeated Ravana.

HOW TO ATTAIN *NIRVANA/MOKSHA*

According to our scriptures (*Taittiriya Samhita and Shatapatha Brahmana*), gratitude should be an integral part of our lives because we come to this world carrying five debts that we need to repay before we can achieve *nirvana* or *moksha*, which are as follows:

1. *Debt to the Gods* (देव ऋण): There is much to be grateful for to God. Our birth, body, family, privileges and good fortune as well as for things that we take for granted. To pay back this debt we need to be thankful in each of our thoughts and actions.
2. *Debt to the rishis* (ऋषि ऋण): Rishis and Rishikas are the wise men and women who have preceded us on this Earth. Would we be able to do what we do if we did not have the knowledge created, discovered and articulated by intellectuals before our times? We can pay back this debt by studying and acquiring knowledge and, if we have the capability, to add to this bank of wisdom and knowledge for future generations.

3. *Debt to our ancestors* (पितृ ऋण): We owe this debt to our ancestors and our parents for the simple (or maybe complex) gift of life that they have given us. Our birth also gives us the unique opportunity of being made the trustees of Mother Earth for our time here, to be passed onto the next generation. We can pay this back by improving or at the very least, preserving, what we have before we hand it over to the next generation.
4. *Debt to fellow human beings* (मनुष्य ऋण): This is the debt we owe to society and our fellow human beings. We can repay this by treating others with respect and being of service to them.
5. *Debt to the five elements* (भूत ऋण): The five elements we owe this debt to are earth, water, fire, air and space. Once we recognize this, we can understand that we can repay this debt by looking after all life on earth, including animals and plants.

Gratitude and appreciation are necessary for a better life as they dissolve hatred, hurt and sadness, healing our disturbed states of mind and restoring self-respect, confidence and security.

Gratitude is a feeling that comes from within when we think of all the good that has happened in our lives. Most of us tend to remember and recall the negative things that have transpired in our lives because they leave the deepest impressions on our minds. It is a good practice to sit down every evening and write down all the good things that have happened to us during the day, as well as the people responsible for such good events. Engaging in this exercise regularly will gradually deepen our appreciation for gratitude and the individuals we should be thankful for.

The next step is appreciation. Once we know who we are grateful to, we need to take the next step and show our appreciation to them. This could be in the form of words or deeds. A sincere word or act of appreciation will go a long way to build and strengthen our bonds.

Gratitude and appreciation could also lead us to understanding forgiveness.

GRATITUDE IN THE WORKPLACE

For deeper connections with each other as well as with the work we are doing every day, we need to express gratitude more often.

1. *Gratitude acknowledges people, not talent:* Many people want appreciation beyond the usual 'you've done a good job', a term we hear so often at work. When leaders appreciate people, they convey the message that leaders are approachable. Leaders need to appreciate and show gratitude for skills beyond the workplace, such as a person who might be a great writer or musician or have any other skill. Soft perquisites, such as flexible work arrangements, are another way to show gratitude for hard work. Similar gestures could have a positive impact on the team's productivity and happiness.
2. *Gratitude creates better leaders:* Work can be stressful for some people. Expressing gratitude can help in managing stress. Gratitude can translate into better engagement at work and more productive interactions. According to a study, employees are 50 per cent more

successful when leaders show gratitude for their efforts.
3. *Gratitude has something for everyone:* When considering gratitude in the workplace, it's important to remember that not everyone wants to be appreciated in the usual way. Some employees may love public praise while others may seek something else. We are all unique and it is the leader's task to recognize these differences and express gratitude accordingly.
4. *Gratitude builds relationships:* Gratitude is a way to strengthen relationships with others at the workplace. A simple 'thank you' can often work wonders.
5. *Gratitude has a positive impact on company culture:* Company culture is a huge factor when it comes to employee retention and recruiting top talent. In a company that practises gratitude, the workforce is generally happier and more productive.

One of the greatest things about expressing gratitude is that it is contagious.

Students should be grateful to their gurus/teachers, spouses to each other and parents to their children. It is far more effective to praise others and appreciate what we have than to find fault and complain about what we don't!

A young man once tried the above practice on his rather gruff employer, whose heart melted when he heard the words, 'One of the things that I appreciate most about you, sir, is your brilliance as an inventor. You have so much to teach me.'

After saying that and more, the youth urged the astonished elder to pass on the voicing of appreciation to another person. The man sat with his son that same evening and awkwardly told him how much he appreciated his only son's many fine qualities. 'I never take time to share these things. I tend to keep to myself and be demanding and harsh because of the pressures of work. But please know that I do love you.'

The youth began sobbing and confessed, 'Father, thank you for making me feel good. I was in a dark place and was planning to end my life as I thought nobody cared about me. Now I know that I have you, who loves and appreciates me.' We never know how much difference our appreciation could make.

To prepare yourself for expressing gratitude, stand in front of a mirror and make eye contact with your own reflection. Then say aloud as if speaking to another person, 'I am grateful to you and appreciate your being in my life.' Then describe to yourself all the good you have done over the past five years. You can read from your list of goodness that you made earlier. You will soon see the reflection in the mirror soften and begin to smile as it absorbs the happy feeling of your appreciation. Once this art is perfected between you and your reflection, you can begin to appreciate others in the same way.

Don't be shy. No one is shy when angry. Why be shy when we are happy and grateful?

MANAGEMENT MANTRAS

Gratitude is a powerful emotion that has the ability to impact an individual's life in numerous ways. It is an appreciation of what one has and an acknowledgement of the good things in life. This positive emotion not only has the potential to improve one's personal life but also holds immense relevance for managers in the professional world. But why is gratitude crucial for managers and how can it help them become better leaders?

Gratitude can help build positive relationships with employees. When a manager shows gratitude for the work performed by their employees, it helps to create a positive work environment. When employees feel appreciated and valued, they are more likely to be motivated and engaged in their work. Furthermore, showing gratitude towards employees fosters trust and respect, which is essential for building healthy relationships in the workplace. Managers who cultivate an environment of gratitude and positivity can foster a sense of community and belonging, ultimately improving employee satisfaction and retention.

Another reason why gratitude is relevant for managers is that it can lead to increased creativity and innovation. When employees feel appreciated, they are more likely to bring new ideas and solutions to the table. Additionally, gratitude helps employees focus on the positives and look at challenges as opportunities for growth. This positive outlook can result in employees taking on more responsibility and pushing themselves to new levels of creativity and innovation.

Moreover, gratitude can help reduce stress and increase happiness in the workplace. When employees are grateful, they are more likely to experience positive emotions and a sense of well-being. This can have a positive impact on their mental health, which is especially important at a time when work-related stress is on the rise. Furthermore, when employees feel happy, they are more likely to be productive and motivated, which is a win–win situation for both the employees and the company.

Gratitude is a crucial aspect of leadership for managers.

It helps build positive relationships with employees, leads to increased creativity and innovation, reduces stress and increases happiness and ultimately helps create a positive work environment. Managers who are grateful are more likely to be effective leaders and achieve success in their careers. Therefore, it is essential for managers to develop and cultivate gratitude in their daily lives and the workplace.

DUTY

श्रेयान्स्वधर्मो विगुण: परधर्मात्स्वनुष्ठितात्।
स्वधर्मे निधनं श्रेय: परधर्मो भयावह:॥

It is better to perform one's duty, even if in a faulty way,
instead of performing someone else's duty perfectly.
In fact, it is preferable to lay down your life
while discharging your duty than follow
someone else's path that is fraught with danger.

—*Bhagavad Gita, Chapter 3, Verse 35*

In our scriptures, dharma primarily means duty and can be defined as the way of righteousness, religious practices and fulfilment of duty. From this perspective, everything we do is an act of worship and faith.

The subject of dharma or duty has been discussed in the Dharmashastras, which are as follows:

- *Manusmriti*
- *Yajnvalkya Smriti*
- *Naradasmriti*
- *Vishnu Smriti*

It is further believed that every individual must perform their duty efficiently for the welfare of society, as then only peace and order will prevail.

TEN IMPORTANT DUTIES

The Vedas and Dharmashastras outline 10 important duties that need to be followed. It is important to perform these duties, which are as follows:

1. *Duty towards self*: Duty towards ourselves can be divided into duties towards the body, mind and soul. This will lead to health, strength, mental clarity, purity and spiritual transformation. Our purpose is to improve and maintain our physical, mental and spiritual well-being.

    उद्धरेदात्मनात्मानं नात्मानमवसादयेत्।
    आत्मैव ह्यात्मनो बन्धुरात्मैव रिपुरात्मनः।।
       —*Bhagavad Gita, Chapter 6, Verse 5*

    It means that one should uplift oneself through the power of one's mind and shouldn't debase oneself because our minds can be our friends as well as enemies. Therefore, we must not indulge in any action that could lead to our moral and spiritual downfall.
2. *Duty towards God*: God exists within us. If we do not feed ourselves, we become weak. Similarly, we risk being more negative in life if we feed our negativity bias. It is

therefore important to cultivate positive thinking as our duty towards God, which we can achieve through performing good deeds and ensuring good conduct.

3. *Duty towards our ancestors*: We owe a debt of gratitude towards our ancestors. According to the Vedas, the souls of our ancestors live in the ancestral world until their karma is completed. Our scriptures believe that by doing good deeds, living virtuously, performing rituals and making our ancestors offerings of food, their descendants can prolong their stay and grant them better lives in their next birth. This is called *pitryajna* or sacrifice for the ancestors.

The Vedas state that this is an important duty of human beings towards their ancestors. If our ancestors are happy, they will also bless us and help us attain peace and prosperity on earth. By serving them, we can repay the karmic debt we owe to them.

Lord Rama's duty in the *Ramayana* is first to his father, which is an extension of his future role in the kingdom. He respects the vow given by his father, King Dasharatha, to his wife Kaikeyi, which seeks to banish Rama for 14 years. Sita's duty is first to her husband, which also extends to the duty she must serve in the future to the kingdom.

Then there's Shravana Kumara from the *Ramayana*. He was the duty-bound son of his blind parents. As he couldn't afford to take them on a pilgrimage by any other means, he placed each of his parents in a basket and tied the baskets to the ends of a bamboo pole so that he could carry them over his shoulders. Anyone who looks after their parents in old age is often referred to as the modern-day Shravana Kumara.

In the *Mahabharata*, Bhishma Pitamaha (also known as Devavrata) vowed a life of celibacy and renounced the throne for his father's pleasure and happiness.

4. *Duty towards progeny*: Our scriptures believe that it is our duty to work for our progeny from the time they are conceived. Parents have an obligation to perform all the sacraments for their children, educate them (either personally or with the help of learned teachers), teach them their duties and responsibilities, inculcate in them good values and help them become virtuous individuals.

At the time of death, they are also expected to pass on their good name, qualities, strengths and abilities to their children through prayers and rituals.

In the *Ramayana*, Lakshmana, realizing that his older brother Lord Rama has been exiled, decides that he would accompany his older brother and sister-in-law with the sole duty of protecting them. He plays a significant role in the journey and the war with Ravana. Lord Rama's younger brother Bharata, who was to be anointed the King based on the wishes of his mother, refuses the coronation and decides that he will serve the kingdom in the name of his older brother for 14 years till it is time for the banishment to be over. Bharata said that only Lord Rama is eligible to rule, being the eldest son of their family. Bharata ruled the kingdom by placing Lord Rama's slippers on the throne.

अहंकारकृतश्चैव सर्वें निरयगामिन:।
परावमानी पुरुषो भविता निरयोपग:।।
—*The Mahabharata, Book 12, Chapter 190, Verse 5*

It means that where there is truth, there is dharma; where there is dharma, there is light; and where there is light, there is happiness. Conversely, where there is falsehood, there is adharma; where there is adharma, there is darkness; and where there is darkness, there is sorrow.[*]

It is believed that Lord Rama was so happy with Lakshmana that he said in their next birth, Rama would be his younger brother. It is believed that Lakshmana was born as Balarama in the *Mahabharata* while Lord Rama was born as his younger brother Lord Krishna.

In the *Mahabharata*, Yudhishthira did not fulfil his duty towards his progeny when he gambled with Duryodhana and Shakuni. After losing all his wealth, Yudhishthira gambled and lost all four of his brothers and their wife Draupadi. When asked what gave him the authority to gamble away his brothers and wife, all that he did was hang his head in shame. But the deed had to be done and all of them had to leave their kingdom and lead life as ascetics in the forest. Once again, this demonstrated how Yudhishthira failed but his brothers and Draupadi lived up to their duty.

5. *Duty towards fellow humans*: We cannot live selfishly. Our life, identity, power, abilities, strengths, riches and enjoyment come from Him. Therefore, in our scriptures, charity is one of the highest virtues. In fact, it is the only virtue that Lord Brahma specifically taught to humans at the beginning of creation for their peace and happiness.

---

[*]'Ideals and Values/Truth & Honesty', https://www.hindupedia.com/en/Ideals_and_Values/Truth_&_Honesty.

Service to humanity is considered service to God. We have an obligation to help the poor and needy, weak and disabled and mendicants, monks and ascetics. We are also expected to serve the guests who visit our homes and educate those who approach us with a request to gain knowledge.

For example, Lord Rama, after defeating Ravana, handed over the throne of Lanka to Ravana's younger brother Vibhishana.

6. *Duty towards other living beings*: Since all living beings possess a soul and are manifestations of God, we have an obligation to show compassion towards all living beings, practise non-violence and avoid harming and hurting anyone, except in self-defence. It is also expected that all living beings will be fed to enable them to survive and flourish.

Animals are not only treated with consideration but are also traditionally worshipped. Many deities have either animal forms and features or use animals as their vehicles. Plants are also treated as living beings.

As Ravana was flying back to Lanka after kidnapping Sita, Jatayu tried to stop him to rescue Sita. Ravana, after a fight, cut off both of Jatayu's wings, who then fell on Earth, grievously injured. With his dying breath, when he narrated to Lord Rama how he failed to save Sita, Lord Rama told him, 'You have actually won. You are victorious because it is not the result but your effort that I appreciate.' Lord Rama then conducted the funeral rites for Jatayu and said 'Today I will perform your funeral rites. I will do it as a son does for his father.'

He then told Lakshmana, 'My dear brother, today is

the most painful day of my life not only because Sita has been abducted but also because of the death of Jatayu. He has rendered a great service to me.'

7. *Duty towards society*: Like all responsible citizens, we are also expected to protect and preserve the institutions of family, caste, community or tradition and ensure there is no chaos and confusion.

    Our scriptures declare that whenever society is in decline and evil is on the rise due to our failure to contain it, God himself manifests upon the Earth to restore dharma or He may manifest His aspects, emanations, demigods and associate powers for the same purpose.

    During normal times we are expected to do it in our individual capacity as the upholders of dharma.

8. *Moral duties*: Every human being has an obligation to practise virtue and uphold the divine laws. We must cultivate purity and discernment.

    Some important moral duties are the study and recitation of scriptures, prayers, worship, rituals, sacrifices, devotion, self-restraint, purity, moral discipline, discernment, resolve, good works and the practice of virtues such as non-violence, truthfulness, refraining from theft and non-covetousness.

    Other duties include respecting elders, parents and teachers, taking care of old and aged members of the family, helping children grow up and avoiding the cardinal sins, namely, lust, anger, pride, envy and delusion.

9. *Professional duties*: All of us are obliged to perform duties and responsibilities that come with power, position and authority. It is important to perform our work based on

the responsibilities that have been entrusted to us.

Those in leadership positions have to act fairly and impartially without falling for temptations and selfishness. Those who become spiritual teachers or take up priesthood functions must live virtuously and spread the knowledge of dharma. Traders and merchants have to practice their professions without lying, cheating and deceiving. Similarly, everyone should follow the rules that apply to them and do their part in serving others.

10. *Duties towards other faiths*: We are expected to respect faiths different from us and live in harmony with them.

    For example, Hinduism clearly affirms that the paths to God are many and that all paths lead to Him. Hence, fanaticism and intolerance are completely ruled out.

    As a practicing Hindu, I not only have a right to choose what I believe in but also have an obligation to defend my faith if necessary. Hindu Gods are an excellent example. They are the most benign and compassionate beings, and yet each is a warrior who will not hesitate to fight the demons if the situation so demands.

∞

The profundity of the concept of duty in our scriptures provides a holistic understanding of our place in the universe. Encompassing more than just obligations, dharma weaves a tapestry of righteousness, justice and moral order, and forms the very core of individual, social and cosmic existence. Our scriptures place an emphasis on dharma as the guiding principle of human behaviour.

Every person has their own *svadharma*, or personal duty. This duty is determined by a combination of factors like age, caste, gender, profession, etc. On a grand scale, dharma ensures the order of the cosmos. The Gods have their dharmas, as do the elements of nature. Every component of the universe, from the smallest creature to the mightiest deity, follows a preordained path of duty to maintain harmony.

Jains believe in five major vows: Ahimsa (non-violence), *Satya* (truth), *Asteya* (non-stealing), *Brahmacharya* (chastity) and *Aparigraha* (non-attachment). Adhering to these vows is seen as the fundamental duty of every Jain.

Sikhism emphasizes three primary duties or pillars: *Naam Japna* (chanting the Divine Name), *Kirat Karni* (earning an honest living) and *Vand Chakna* (sharing with others, especially those who are less fortunate). One of the essential duties in Sikhism is to engage in selfless service (*Seva*). This can be through physical actions, such as serving in the community kitchen (*Langar*) or through other forms of assistance and charity.

It is important that in performing our duties, we should remain selfless and offer the fruit of such actions to God, who is the source and cause of all.

MANAGEMENT MANTRAS

Duty is a fundamental aspect of a manager's role, encompassing the responsibilities and obligations necessary for successfully leading a team. Duty is essential in the management of any organization, as it helps in ensuring that goals are met, tasks are completed and employees are motivated and engaged.

The primary duty of a manager is to provide clear and effective leadership. This involves setting clear goals and objectives, communicating expectations and establishing guidelines for performance and behaviour. A manager must also lead by example, demonstrating the values and behaviours they expect of their team.

Another key duty of a manager is to foster a positive and productive work environment. This requires creating an atmosphere of trust, collaboration and support where employees feel valued and are encouraged to bring their best to the job. Additionally, a manager must address any conflicts or issues that arise in the workplace and work to resolve them in a fair and equitable manner.

A manager also has the duty to ensure the professional development of their team members. This includes providing training and development opportunities, mentorship and feedback, and creating opportunities for employees to grow and advance within the organization.

Finally, a manager must take responsibility for the financial performance of their team and the organization. This involves developing budgets, monitoring expenses and ensuring that resources are used effectively and efficiently. A manager must also be accountable for the results of their team and take appropriate actions to address any issues or challenges that arise.

CAREER CHALLENGES

उद्धरेदात्मनात्मानं नात्मानमवसादयेत्।
आत्मैव ह्यात्मनो बन्धुरात्मैव रिपुरात्मनः।।

Lift up the self by the Self
And don't let the self droop down,
For the Self is the self's only friend
And the self is the Self's only foe.

—*Bhagavad Gita, Chapter 6, Verse 5*

Careers have always been an important aspect of human life, as they determine an individual's status, financial stability and social identity.

Our scriptures consider careers as an integral part of human life and offer valuable insights into how one should approach their professional life.

One of the most significant teachings in Hinduism is the concept of dharma, which refers to one's moral and ethical duty. This concept is central to the Hindu view of careers as it emphasizes that an individual's chosen career should be in line with their dharma. This means that an individual should choose a career that aligns with their innate qualities and skills, values and beliefs. The idea is that by fulfilling one's dharma, an individual will attain inner peace, happiness and fulfilment.

The *Bhagavad Gita* mentions the importance of dharma in a person's life. Lord Krishna counsels Arjuna on the importance of fulfilling his dharma, even if it means engaging in battle. This teaching highlights the importance of fulfilling one's responsibilities, regardless of the circumstances.

The scriptures also stress on the importance of working with dedication and devotion, regardless of the type of work one is engaged in. According to the scriptures, even menial work performed with dedication and devotion is considered sacred. This teaching reflects the Hindu belief that work itself is a form of worship and that it is the attitude and approach towards work that determines its worth and value.

The scriptures view careers as a means of serving society and contributing to its well-being. This is reflected in the concept of seva, which refers to selfless service. By serving others, an individual can attain spiritual growth and fulfilment. This idea is particularly relevant to careers in fields such as healthcare, social work and education, where individuals can serve others and contribute to society in meaningful ways.

Another important teaching is the concept of karma, which refers to the law of cause and effect. According to this teaching, an individual's actions and decisions determine their future experiences and outcomes. In the context of careers, this means that one's actions and decisions in their professional life will have both good and bad consequences. By engaging in ethical and responsible practices, an individual can attract positive karma, which will bring success and fulfilment in their career.

The idea of moksha or liberation is central to one's spiritual journey. Moksha refers to the ultimate goal of human life, which is to attain freedom from the cycle of birth and death, reaching a state of consciousness beyond the physical world. Careers are viewed as a means of achieving moksha by fulfilling one's dharma and serving society. By doing so, an individual can attain spiritual growth and fulfilment, which is essential for attaining moksha.

The importance of dedication and devotion in work, the idea of serving society, the law of karma and the ultimate goal of moksha are all teachings that offer guidance on how to approach one's career in a meaningful and fulfilling way. By following these teachings, we can attain success, happiness and fulfilment in our professional lives, and contribute to society in a positive and meaningful way.

CHALLENGES IN OUR WORK LIFE

Difficulty in choosing the right path

Our scriptures emphasize the importance of finding our true calling, which is often referred to as *svadharma*. The *Bhagavad Gita* states that we should perform our duties without attachment to the fruits of their labour. This means that we should choose a career that aligns with our values and abilities rather than being driven by external factors such as wealth or social status. The key is to find a career that brings joy and fulfilment and to stay true to it, even in the face of challenges.

Lack of clarity about our goals and aspirations

We are often confused and confronted with uncertainty about which path to take and what actions to pursue. The *Gita* addresses this challenge by emphasizing the importance of self-knowledge and introspection. We must examine our own nature and tendencies to understand our strengths and weaknesses, and to determine what kind of work is most suitable for us. We must also cultivate a sense of detachment from external factors such as rewards and recognition, instead focussing on performing our duties with sincerity and dedication.

Managing the struggle for success and recognition

The scriptures emphasize that success should not be measured by external factors such as wealth or power but rather by our own inner peace and happiness. The *Bhagavad Gita* states that we should not be attached to success or failure and that we should strive for excellence in our work, regardless of the outcome. This helps to remove the pressure of constantly seeking external validation, allowing us to focus on the joy of the work itself.

Lack of motivation or enthusiasm

The Upanishads address this challenge by emphasizing the importance of finding our purpose or *dharma*. Aligning our work with our innermost values and aspirations can provide a sense of fulfilment and inspiration. The Upanishads also advice individuals to cultivate a positive attitude and to view their work as a service to others, rather than as a means of self-gratification.

Lack of ethical standards or conflicts between personal values and organizational culture

The *Bhagavad Gita* and the Upanishads stress upon the importance of ethical conduct and moral values. We should adhere to a set of universal principles such as honesty, integrity and compassion, and these principles should guide our actions and decisions in the workplace. It is also advisable to maintain a sense of detachment from the fruits of our actions and to focus instead on doing what is right and just.

Dealing with difficult people and situations in the workplace

The importance of being compassionate and non-violent, even in the face of adversity, is discussed several times in our scriptures. The *Mahabharata* states that one should never use violence, even against those who are evil, as this only perpetuates the cycle of violence. Instead, we should use wisdom and non-violent communication to resolve conflicts and build bridges with others. Mahatma Gandhi epitomized this form of dealing with difficult people.

Finding balance in work and personal life

Our scriptures emphasize the importance of finding a balance between work and personal life—not allowing one to take over the other. *Manusmriti* states that we should divide our time between work, family and spiritual pursuits, and not allow any one area to dominate our life. This helps to maintain a healthy work-life balance, which is crucial for both personal and professional success. It is also advisable to prioritize our physical, emotional and spiritual well-being, and to make time for activities such as meditation, yoga and other practices that promote balance and harmony.

Dealing with failures and setbacks in our career

The importance of perseverance and resilience in the face of adversity is taught to us from a young age. The *Ramayana* states that we should never give up, even in the face of defeat, and that we should continue to strive towards our goals, no matter how difficult the journey may be. This helps build inner strength and resilience and allows one to bounce back from setbacks and failures.

Each one of us has a unique dharma that we must fulfil in our lives. This dharma is determined by various factors such as our innate qualities, social status and stage of life.

The key is to find one's true calling, strive for excellence, be compassionate and non-violent, find balance in work and personal life and persevere in the face of adversity. By following these principles, one can not only achieve success in their career but also attain inner peace and happiness, which is the ultimate goal of Hindu philosophy.

MANAGEMENT MANTRAS

In today's fast-paced and highly competitive business world, managers face numerous challenges as they strive to meet their career objectives. Whether it's handling difficult employees, overcoming unexpected setbacks or adapting to rapidly changing market conditions, managers must possess the right skills and mindset to navigate through various challenges that come their way.

The first lesson for managers facing career challenges is to stay positive and maintain a growth mindset. The ability to stay positive and focus on finding solutions instead of dwelling on problems is essential for success. Challenges can be overwhelming and managers may feel like giving up. However, with a positive attitude, they can overcome obstacles, learn from them and come out stronger. Adopting a growth mindset also means being open to feedback, taking calculated risks and embracing change.

The second lesson is to be proactive and take charge of one's career. Managers must take responsibility for their career growth and development. They should set clear goals, identify the skills they need to develop and take steps to acquire them. This may involve seeking out new learning opportunities, taking on challenging assignments or seeking feedback from colleagues and mentors. By taking proactive steps to develop themselves, managers can position themselves for success, regardless of the challenges they face.

The third lesson is to build strong relationships with colleagues and stakeholders. In any business setting, success depends on the ability to work well with others. Managers must build strong relationships with their team members, superiors and clients. This requires effective communication skills, active listening and empathy. By building trust and respect with others, managers can cultivate a collaborative work environment where everyone can contribute their best efforts.

The fourth lesson is to develop resilience and the ability to adapt to change. No matter how well-prepared managers may be, unexpected challenges will always arise. In such situations, managers need to be resilient and adaptable. This means being able to quickly bounce back from setbacks, staying calm under pressure and being willing to adjust plans as needed. By developing resilience and adaptability, managers can face any challenge with confidence.

The fifth and final lesson is to practise self-care and maintain a healthy work–life balance. Managers face high levels of stress and pressure and it's important to take care of themselves both physically and mentally. This may involve taking breaks during the workday, getting enough sleep and engaging in activities that promote relaxation and well-being. Prioritizing self-care will enable managers to perform their best, even when faced with challenging situations.

Managers face numerous career challenges in today's business world. However, by adopting a positive attitude, taking proactive steps to develop themselves, building strong relationships, developing resilience and adaptability and practising self-care, they can overcome these challenges and achieve their career goals. By incorporating these essential lessons into their daily practices, managers can thrive in their roles and achieve long-term success.

LISTENING

You may sit down and listen to me by the hour every day, but if you do not practice, you will not get one step further. It all depends on practice.*

—*Swami Vivekananda*

Jiddu Krishnamurti, the renowned Indian philosopher and speaker, emphasized the importance of listening in his teachings. He believed that listening is not just about hearing the words being spoken but an active and attentive process that involves understanding, empathy and curiosity.

According to Krishnamurti, true listening can only happen when one is free from their preconceptions, biases and judgements. He argued that listening with these prejudices prevents genuine understanding as we are not open to new perspectives and ideas. Therefore, to listen effectively, one

---

*Swami Vivekananda, *Raja Yoga*, Brentano's, New York, 1920.

must be present and fully engaged in the moment without any distractions or thoughts clouding the mind.

Krishnamurthi further argued that true listening requires one to be non-judgemental, because when one judges, they are no longer listening but instead are thinking about their own opinions and evaluation. He believed that when we listen without judgment, we can truly understand and connect with the speaker, and in doing so, gain a deeper insight into the world.[*]

Listening, also known as *shravana*, is considered one of the most important qualities in Hinduism. It is believed to be a path towards attaining inner peace, knowledge and enlightenment. Our scriptures, such as the Vedas, Upanishads, *Bhagavad Gita* and Puranas, emphasize the importance of listening in our spiritual journey.

In Hinduism, listening is considered to be a form of devotion. It involves listening to the teachings of the scriptures, the words of the Guru and the sounds of nature. Listening with an open heart and mind can bring immense peace, clarity and joy to the listener. It is believed that when we listen deeply and attentively, we can learn and understand the secrets of the universe and can attain self-realization.

The Vedas, considered the oldest and most sacred Hindu scriptures, describe the power of listening. In the *Rig Veda*, it is said that the highest form of knowledge is attained through listening. The Vedas also emphasize the importance of listening to the teachings of the Guru, who is considered a messenger of God and the source of divine wisdom.

---

[*]'The Art of Listening: Dialogue 10 San Diego, California, USA, 22 February 1974', https://www.jkrishnamurti.org/content/art-listening.

The Upanishads, a collection of ancient Hindu texts, provide deeper insights into the importance of listening. They emphasize that listening to the truth and living it can bring inner peace and happiness.

In the *Bhagavad Gita*, Lord Krishna instructs Arjuna to listen to his teachings and follow them to attain enlightenment.

Chanakya's thoughts on listening have been widely revered and quoted over the centuries, and his ideas continue to be relevant even today.

Chanakya believed that listening was a crucial skill for anyone who wanted to be successful in life. He stated that silence was a true friend that never betrays and that the ability to listen and be silent was essential for understanding and learning. By being quiet and paying attention, one could gain valuable insights into the thoughts and opinions of others, and this knowledge could be used to make informed decisions.

In Chanakya's view, listening was also an important tool for building relationships. He believed that people who listened attentively were more likely to be respected and trusted by others and that this could be an invaluable asset in any personal or professional situation. By being a good listener, one could create strong, positive relationships that would last a lifetime.

Furthermore, Chanakya emphasized the importance of being open-minded when listening. He believed that the ability to listen to different perspectives and ideas was crucial for personal growth and development. By being open to new ideas and approaches, one could learn and grow in ways that would otherwise not be possible.

In Hinduism, listening is not just about hearing the

words, but about understanding the meaning behind them. It involves an active process of questioning, contemplating and applying the teachings to our lives. Our scriptures also emphasize that listening should be done with a pure heart and mind, free from any distractions or biases.

Listening to the sounds of nature is also considered an important aspect of Hindu spirituality. Hindu scriptures describe the sounds of nature as sacred and believe that they hold within them the secrets of the universe. The sounds of birds, rivers, oceans and forests are considered to be the manifestation of the Divine, and listening to them can bring peace, harmony and happiness to the listener.

Our scriptures also emphasize the importance of listening to the inner voice. This inner voice is considered to be the voice of the Divine and can guide one towards the truth and ultimate reality. Listening to the inner voice requires quieting the mind and being attentive to our thoughts and feelings.

Listening also plays an important role in Hindu rituals and ceremonies. Hindu prayers and hymns are often accompanied by music and singing, which are believed to purify the mind and soul. Listening to sacred music can bring joy and peace to the listener and is considered a form of devotion to the Divine.

MANAGEMENT MANTRAS

Managers must possess effective listening skills. It not only helps to foster positive relationships with employees but also leads to improved problem-solving and decision-making.

Some key reasons why managers need to listen effectively are as follows:

Better understanding

Listening actively allows managers to gain a deeper understanding of their employees' thoughts, concerns and needs. By listening carefully, they can identify areas where they can help or provide support.

Improved relationships

Employees feel valued when their managers listen to them and show interest in what they have to say. This, in turn, leads to better relationships between managers and employees, which can improve morale and motivation.

Enhanced problem solving

Managers who listen are better equipped to identify and solve problems. When employees feel heard and their concerns are addressed, they are more likely to collaborate and come up with creative solutions.

Improved decision making

Effective listening enables managers to gather all relevant information before making a decision. It also allows them to consider different perspectives, leading to more informed and effective decisions.

Increased productivity

When employees feel valued and their concerns are addressed, they are more likely to be productive and committed to their work. This can lead to improved performance and increased success for the company.

By taking the time to listen, managers can improve

relationships, solve problems, make informed decisions and increase productivity. By prioritizing this skill, managers can have a positive impact on their team and the organization as a whole.

SAHASRARA CHAKRA

Connecting Businesses with the People

The seventh and final is the Sahasrara or Crown Chakra, which fosters a sense of unity with the Divine and the Universe. When balanced, it allows us to experience states of heightened awareness, mindfulness and encourages us to seek a deeper understanding of our existence and align our actions with a higher purpose.

In Hindu scriptures, there is a Sanskrit phrase, *Vasudhaiva Kutumbakam*, which translates to 'the world is one family'. It emphasizes the interconnectedness of all people and encourages the idea that every human being is part of a larger, global community. The *Rig Veda* and the Upanishads emphasize the importance of treating all human beings as equals and promoting unity among people of different backgrounds.

Diversity promotes the idea that it is a strength and that all people have value and are deserving of respect. It encourages people to embrace their differences and appreciate the unique qualities that each individual brings to the table.

Equity promotes the idea that every human being is entitled to equal rights and opportunities, regardless of their circumstances. It encourages people to work towards creating a more just and equitable society where all individuals have access to the resources they need to succeed.

Inclusion encourages people to create environments that are welcoming and inclusive of all individuals, regardless of their background. It promotes the idea that everyone has a place in society and that everyone should be able to participate fully in all aspects of life.

Diplomacy promotes the idea that cooperation and dialogue are key to resolving conflicts and promoting peace. It encourages people to view their relationships with others in a positive light and to seek mutually beneficial outcomes in all situations.

Legacy is not just material inheritance but the wisdom, values and actions one passes on. The principle of *karma* reinforces the notion that our deeds, both good and bad, leave an enduring impact on our soul and the cosmic order. The ultimate aim is to leave a legacy that aligns with dharma, ensuring spiritual growth and liberation (*moksha*) for oneself and inspiring others towards the same path.

Vasudhaiva Kutumbakam is a powerful concept that has significant implications for diversity, equity, inclusion, diplomacy and legacy. This idea emphasizes the interconnectedness of all people and encourages individuals to treat others with respect and compassion. It promotes a worldview that is inclusive and emphasizes the importance of working towards a more just and equitable society.

In today's increasingly globalized world, this concept is more relevant than ever and can provide a powerful framework for creating a more peaceful and harmonious world, connecting businesses with the people.

DIVERSITY, EQUITY, INCLUSION

विद्याविनयसम्पन्ने ब्राह्मणे गवि हस्तिनि।
शुनि चैव श्वपाके च पण्डिताः समदर्शिनः॥

A wise person perceives the same divine principle
or eternal soul (Atman) in every being,
irrespective of the external differences
or societal designations.

—*Bhagavad Gita, Chapter 5, Verse 18*

The phrase *Vasudhaiva Kutumbakam* (वसुधैव कुटुम्बकम्), translating to 'the world is one family', embodies the basic philosophy of Hinduism.

अयं निजः परो वेति गणना लघुचेतसाम्।
उदारचरितानां तु वसुधैव कुटुम्बकम्॥

—*Maha Upanishad, Chapter 6, Verse 71*

The above verse is engraved in the entrance hall of the Parliament of India and conveys that small-minded individuals see some as kin and others as strangers whereas the wise knows that the world is but one big family. Our scriptures have always referred to the world as one family.

GENDER EQUALITY

Goal 5 of the United Nations' Sustainable Development Goals (SDGs) is gender equality. Further, Goal 10 is reduced inequalities, which has also been written about extensively in our scriptures.

Our scriptures have always treated men and women equally, with Hinduism teaching that the Divine is equally present in all. Prejudice and discrimination against anyone violates this fundamental teaching.

In traditional Indian astronomy, Rishika Arundhati—the wife of one of the seven seers Rishi Vasishtha—is accorded the same status as the seven seers. Together they are identified as the two stars in the twin-star system that are gravitationally bound to each other. In most twin-star systems, one is stationary while the other rotates around it. But Arundhati and Vasishtha travel the cosmos together by orbiting the same centre of mass, thus conveying equality in the relationship between men and women.

Arundhati was given a place in the Saptarshi constellation thousands of years ago. This was well before the world started to realize the importance of diversity, equity and inclusion.

GODDESSES

Goddesses have always been worshipped in our scriptures, which continue till today. The three deities worshipped in different forms across India are Saraswati, Lakshmi and Shakti, linked to the Trimurti (or the trinity of supreme divinity in Hinduism) of Brahma, Vishnu and Shiva, respectively.

Saraswati is the Goddess of Learning. She is usually shown holding a veena (a musical instrument), with a swan beside her. Saraswati is the consort of Brahma. Their son is Manu, the author of *Manusmriti* or the *Laws of Manu*. Saraswati is worshipped for knowledge.

Lakshmi is the Goddess of Wealth. She is normally shown holding lotus flowers, with a pot of money next to her. She is the consort of Vishnu. She is worshipped during festivals like Diwali.

Shakti is the Goddess representing divine feminine energy. She is worshipped as Parvati, the first wife of Shiva. Shakti is also worshipped in other forms—including Durga and Kali.

WOMEN AND EDUCATION

The Vedas offer several insights into the education of women. The *Atharva Veda* particularly supports female empowerment, highlighting that women are an integral aspect of society.

The Vedas also strongly emphasize the education of females. Believing each individual to be equal to the next, Vedic literature not only encourages women and girls to be scholarly but also expresses that parents must ensure their daughters are brought up and educated with great effort and care.

1. इयं शुष्मेभिर्बिसखा इवारुजत्सानु गिरीणां तविषेभिरूर्मिभिः।
   पारावतघ्नीमवसे सुवृक्तिभिः सरस्वतीमा विवासेम धीतिभिः॥
   —*Rig Veda*,* *Book 6, Chapter 61, Verse 2*

This verse praises Saraswati not just as a physical river but, more importantly, as the divine flow of knowledge and inspiration. The verse beautifully juxtaposes the imagery of a river's might and flow with the power

---

*The *Rig Veda Samhita* contains about 10,552 mantras, classified into 10 books called *Mandala*, which are further divided into chapters called *Suktas* made up of verses called *riks*. Similarly, the *Atharva Veda* is divided into *Kandas* comprising *Suktas* that are classified into *Mantras*.

and vastness of wisdom and creativity that Saraswati embodies. The hymn seeks blessings and the ability to dwell in the vast expanse of her divine knowledge and wisdom. The way a river breaks away the mightiest of hills and rocks, with the blessings of Saraswati, a scholarly woman destroys darkness and ignorance from our lives through her intellect. May we be forever grateful to such women through our polite words and noble actions.

2. त्वे विश्वा सरस्वति श्रितायूंषि देव्याम्।
   शुनहोत्रेषु मत्स्व प्रजां देवि दिदिड्ढि न:॥
   —*Rig Veda, Book 2, Chapter 41, Verse 17*

This verse is dedicated to Saraswati, the Goddess of knowledge, music, arts, wisdom and learning. In the Vedic context, Saraswati is also associated with rivers and water, which symbolize purity, fertility and life. The life of the entire society depends upon the intellectual female who provides us with the right knowledge and brings knowledge to all segments of society.

3. ब्रह्मापरंयुज्यतां ब्रह्म पूर्वं ब्रह्मान्ततो मध्यतो ब्रह्म सर्वत:।
   अनाव्याधां देवपुरां प्रपद्य शिवा स्योना पतिलोके वि राज॥
   —*Atharva Veda, Book 14, Chapter 1, Verse 64*

This verse highlights the omnipresence of Brahman, the ultimate reality or universal consciousness, emphasizing that it is everywhere—before, in the middle and at the end. The latter part of the verse speaks of an aspiration to dwell in the pure city (or realm) of divinity and to rule over these domains benevolently.

4. चित्तिरा उपबर्हणं चक्षुरा अभ्यञ्जनम्।
   द्यौर्भूमि: कोश आसीद्यदयात्सूर्या पतिम्॥
   —*Rig Veda, Book 10, Chapter 85, Verse 7*

This verse underscores the idea that marriage is a cosmic event, interlinking individual, social and cosmic orders. It also emphasizes the sacred and divine nature of marriage in the Vedic tradition. Parents, when marrying off their daughter, should give her the gift of knowledge.

WOMEN AND MARRIAGE

The Vedas regard marriage as a union of two equals, where neither partner is given more importance than the other. The Vedas believe that both husband and wife constitute the *griha* or home. In fact, after marriage, the wife is considered to be the *ardhangini*, meaning the other half or her husband's equal partner. The wife also becomes the *samrajni* or the queen of the household and has an equal share in the performance of religious rites. These can also be observed in the following passages:

1. भगस्त्वेतोनयतु हस्तगृह्याश्विना त्वा प्र वहतां रथेन।
   गृहान्गच्छ गृहपत्नीयथासो वशिनी त्वं विदथमा वदासि।।
   —*Atharva Veda, Book 14, Chapter 1, Verse 20*

This verse focuses on domestic life, particularly relating to marriage and setting up a household. The mention of the *Ashvins*, the twin horsemen deities in Vedic texts, suggests divine intervention or blessing for the journey of life or marital life. The Ashvins are often associated with health, well-being and protection. The verse also speaks about instructions to a woman to enter her new home as the 'mistress of the home' and to adhere to established norms or customs.

2. अमोऽहमस्मिसा त्वं सामाहमस्म्यृक्त्वं द्यौरहं पृथिवी त्वम्।
   ताविह सं भवावप्रजामा जनयावहै।।
   —*Atharva Veda, Book 14, Chapter 2, Verse 71*

   This verse articulates the interdependence, unity and coexistence of two entities or forces, emphasizing their importance in the greater cosmic order. It underscores the harmony and balance between them and their roles in creation and sustenance. Both the partners are knowledgeable.

3. समानो मन्त्र: समिति: समानी समानं मन: सह चित्तमेषाम्।
   समानं मन्त्रमभि मन्त्रये व: समानेन वो हविषा जुहोमि।।
   —*Rig Veda, Book 10, Chapter 191, Verse 3*

   The *Rig Veda* often speaks about the physical, mental and spiritual unity of people. In this verse, there is a profound sense of collective consciousness being expressed. The prayer emphasizes that just as the speech (*mantra*), assembly (*samiti*) and the minds (*manah*) of the people are one, their goals and aspirations should also align. This unity is essential for the collective good of the community.

   At its core, this verse emphasizes the importance of unity, harmony, equal participation and collective well-being.

These mantras are shared with women as they are shared with men. May both their thoughts, too, be harmonious. May their assemblies be open to all without discrimination, which means that the mind and consciousness should also be harmonious. Men and women are provided with equal powers to absorb the learnings of these mantras.

The fact that women and men are seen as equals in the eyes of *dharma* reflects the inclusiveness of the Vedas. Our scriptures emphasize that a spirit of cooperation and appreciation between men and women is what leads to societal progression.

WOMEN AND MOTHERHOOD

Vedic dharma states that each woman must be accorded the highest respect and honour. She must be respected as we would respect our own mother.

The status of women as a mother is bestowed not only upon mothers but all women, regardless of age, religion, caste or creed. The Vedas believe that women are born with the ability to civilize society merely by their presence, which can be seen as follows:

1. अहं रुद्राय धनुरा तनोमि ब्रह्मद्विषे शरावे हन्तवा उ।
   अहं जनाय समदं कृणोम्यहं द्यावापृथिवी आ विवेश॥

   I make the man bow to me, who is all-powerful; my womb, the source of all creation, bears the father on its head.

   —*Rig Veda, Book 10, Chapter 125, Verse 6*

This verse celebrates the feminine as the source of creation, signifying her vital role in the process of creation and continuation of life.

2. यत्र नार्यस्तु पूज्यन्ते रमन्ते तत्र देवताः।
   यत्रैतास्तु न पूज्यन्ते सर्वास्तत्राफलाः क्रियाः॥

   Where women are honoured, there the Gods rejoice; but where they are not honoured, all work becomes fruitless.

   —*Manusmriti, Discourse 3, Verse 56*

This verse emphasizes the importance and respect that should be accorded to women in society.

3. अहं राष्ट्री संगमनी वसूनां चिकितुषी प्रथमा यज्ञियानाम्।
तां मा देवा व्यदधुः पुरुत्रा भूरिस्थात्रां भूर्यावेशयन्तीम्।।

   I am the queen, the gatherer-up of treasures, most thoughtful, first of those who merit worship.

   —*Rig Veda, Book 10, Chapter 125, Verse 3*

This verse is an assertion of the feminine principle as both a leader and a central figure deserving of worship.

4. मातृदेवो भव।

   Let your mother be a God to you.

   —*Taittiriya Upanishad, Book 1, Chapter 11, Verse 2*

This verse underscores the high regard one should have for their mother, equating her with the Divine.

5. उत स्या नो दिवा मतिरदितिरूत्या गमत्।
सा शंताति मयस्करदप स्निधः।।

   —*Rig Veda, Book 8, Chapter 18, Verse 7*

This verse invokes Aditi, an ancient Vedic Goddess, considered the mother of all Gods and the personification of the infinite. It asks for her protection, guidance and benevolence. Aditi is often invoked for her nurturing and protective qualities. It could also be interpreted as 'may the woman of the house be respected as Mother Nature every day so that she provides us with peace and eradicates all hatred, negative values and heresies from society.'

STREEDHAN

A widespread social evil that has plagued modern society is the dowry system. This has caused a lot of challenges to women and their parents.

Parents should voluntarily provide their daughters with a share of property in their name to ensure financial security for an independent life once they leave their parental homes, i.e. once they are married.

The concept of *streedhan*, or wealth of the woman, exists only in India—a concept that has been passed down over centuries from the Dharmashastras. The following are considered to be *streedhan*:

1. Gifts received by the bride before the nuptial fire.
2. Gifts received by the bride during the bridal procession.
3. Gifts received by the bride as a token of love from her in-laws.
4. Gifts received by the bride from her parents and siblings.
5. Gifts and bequests from strangers during maidenhood.

It is the right of women to claim their wealth at any time and use it in whichever way they want. *Streedhan* is the wealth and other belongings that a woman brings from her parent's home before, during or after marriage.

Streedhan exclusively belongs to the woman and no court will take this into account when deciding upon a separation of assets between a man and a woman.

Several legal interpretations exist for *streedhan* and the

above points have been presented only as an illustration. In the event of a problem, it would be best to consult a lawyer.

My objective of discussing this topic is only to ensure that the concept of *streedhan* is understood by the reader.

INCLUSION

Inclusion of people with disabilities has always been a topic of discussion and most organizations have understood the need for inclusion, adapting their businesses to accommodate the needs of individuals who are physically challenged.

Our scriptures have always understood the need for this inclusion, and we see several characters in our scriptures who had a physical challenge and were still in powerful roles or positions of power.

It is evident that people with disabilities participated in society at all levels. There was no discrimination on account of their physical challenges. A few examples are as follows[*]:

1. Ashtavakra

Brahmarshi Ashtavakra was born with eight deformities. Legend has it that while he was in the womb, he had learned the Vedic mantras from his maternal grandfather. One day, his father was chanting the Vedic mantras and he made eight mistakes in the pronunciation. Ashtavakra, from his mother's womb, corrected the mistakes made by his father.

---

[*]Lalit, Samyak, 'Persons with Disability in Hindu Mythology', *WeCapable.com*, 16 January 2021, https://wecapable.com/disability-indian-mythology/.

His father was not able to handle the corrections and cursed the unborn child with eight deformities.

Ashtavakra, despite these deformities, became a respected Rishi and over time, with his knowledge and intelligence, a Brahmarshi. He was the official Guru of King Janaka, father of Goddess Sita.

2. Dhritarashtra

Dhritarashtra, the father of the Kauravas and the uncle of the Pandavas in the *Mahabharata*, was blind. King Vichitravirya died, leaving no heirs from his wives Ambika and Ambalika. His mother, Satyavati, called her other son, Rishi Vyasa to impregnate both Ambika and Ambalika. Ambika was scared when she saw Vyasa and closed her eyes. As a result, her son Dhritarashtra was born blind. Ambalika turned pale, so her son Pandu was weak and sickly. Pandu was crowned the king but died due to a curse.

Dhritarashtra was thereby crowned the king. He was believed to have the strength of one hundred thousand elephants because of a boon given by Vyasa. Even though his role in the *Mahabharata* is controversial as he had the power to stop the war between his sons and nephews but did not, he was a knowledgeable person with an immense commitment to *dharma*, except when it came to anything that favoured his son Duryodhana.

3. Shakuni

The prince of the Kingdom of Gandhara (now in modern Pakistan and Afghanistan), Shakuni, walked with a pronounced limp. He was angered when his sister Gandhari was married to the blind Dhritarashtra. He vowed to destroy the Kuru dynasty because of this affront and made his nephew Duryodhana completely dependent on him. Shakuni played a critical role in the game of dice that the Pandavas lost, after which they were sent into exile for 14 years.

4. Kalidasa

Mahakavi Kalidasa lived in the era of King Vikramaditya. He was one of the nine gems in the King's court.

The daughter of the local king had decided that she would marry a person who was as intelligent as her. She turned down the proposal of a scholar who was selected by her father. The scholar was angered and decided that she had to be taught a lesson by being married to a foolish person.

There was a man who had lost his parents when he was six months old. He had no education and was believed to have poor intellect. He was once cutting the branch of a tree on which he was sitting, though on the wrong side, because of which he too fell. The scholar decided that he had to be the most foolish man.

The scholar managed to present this man as a highly intelligent person who had taken a vow of silence. The princess agreed to marry him but the truth was revealed on the first night and she threw him out of the palace.

On being thrown out, the man decided that he had to acquire knowledge. A Yogi asked him to worship Goddess Kali. He meditated for many days and nights. Goddess Kali, pleased with his devotion and simplicity, blessed him with extraordinary intellect. Thus, Mahakavi Kalidasa was born, which is the poet's pseudonym and not the birth name.

5. Manthara

Manthara, the maid of Queen Kaikeyi from the *Ramayana*, is a well-recognized character. She was born with a hunch and visual impairment.

As a highly trusted maid to a powerful queen, she played a significant role in reminding Kaikeyi about the two vows that King Dasharatha had made to her on the battlefield.

Manthara suggested to Queen Kaikeyi that she should ask for the throne for her son Bharata and exile Lord Rama for 14 years.

6. Vamana

Vamana, the Dwarf, is one of the 10 avatars of Lord Vishnu. It is believed that Vamana went to one of the sacrifices being performed by Bali, the demon king, who had conquered the three worlds after defeating Indra. Vamana asked Bali for land equal to three steps.

Once Bali agreed, Vamana grew in size and covered Heaven and Earth in two steps. To meet his commitment, Bali offered his head for the third step. Lord Vishnu stepped on his head and pushed Bali to the underworld.

Many other instances in our scriptures depict persons with disabilities, such as the charioteer of the Sun God, who was born without a lower body, and Surdas, a devotee of Krishna, who chose to remain blind because he had a vision of Lord Krishna.

MANAGEMENT MANTRAS

Diversity, equity and inclusion (DEI) have become essential aspects of modern business, gaining increasing importance in recent years. In today's fast-paced and highly competitive business environment, companies must be equipped to handle the diverse needs and perspectives of their employees and customers. To achieve this, managers play a critical role in implementing DEI strategies within their organizations.

DEI refers to the creation of a workplace culture that promotes and values diversity in terms of race, ethnicity, gender, age, sexual orientation, religion and other personal characteristics. This not only benefits the individuals who make up an organization but also contributes to the overall success of the company. A diverse workplace leads to greater creativity, innovation and problem-solving ability, as well as improved morale, engagement and retention of employees.

For DEI to be effective, it must be integrated into the company's culture and operations, starting from the top. Managers must take an active role in promoting DEI by leading by example, setting policies and procedures that are inclusive and being mindful of the language they use and the attitudes they display towards different groups.

One of the key responsibilities of managers in promoting DEI is to create an inclusive work environment. This involves recognizing and valuing the unique strengths and perspectives that each employee brings to the table. Managers can foster an inclusive work environment by encouraging open communication, promoting teamwork and actively listening to the concerns and feedback of employees.

Another important aspect of promoting DEI is to provide

diversity and inclusion training for employees. This training should cover topics such as unconscious bias, cultural sensitivity and ways to create an inclusive workplace. This training should be mandatory for all employees, including managers, and should be ongoing to ensure that everyone is up-to-date on the latest DEI best practices.

Managers can further promote DEI by setting diversity goals and actively working towards them. This can involve implementing diversity initiatives, such as mentorship programs, networking events and employee resource groups to promote diversity and help employees feel valued and included. Managers should also regularly review and measure the progress of these initiatives and make any necessary adjustments to ensure they are effective.

In addition to promoting DEI within the workplace, managers can also ensure that the company's products and services are inclusive and accessible to all customers. This can involve conducting market research to understand the needs and perspectives of different customer segments and making any necessary changes to products and services to better serve these customers.

Another important aspect of promoting DEI is to address and eliminate discrimination and bias within the workplace. Managers should have a zero-tolerance policy for discrimination and should provide a safe and supportive environment for employees to report incidents of discrimination. Managers should also ensure that the company has a clear and effective process for investigating and addressing claims of discrimination and that all employees are aware of this process.

Finally, managers should be aware of the legal

requirements and regulations related to DEI. This includes compliance with equal employment opportunity laws, anti-discrimination laws and other regulations that apply to their industry. Managers should stay informed about any changes or updates to these laws and regulations and ensure that their company is in compliance.

DEI is an important aspect of modern business that has far-reaching benefits for both employees and the company as a whole. Managers, through their leadership and commitment, play a critical role in promoting DEI and creating an inclusive workplace culture.

DIPLOMACY

There is some self-interest behind every friendship.
There is no friendship without self-interests.
This is a bitter truth.

—*Chanakya*

In *Mahabharata*, Duryodhana wanted to imprison Lord Krishna to prevent him from meeting the various stakeholders. Dhritarashtra, who normally went along with his older son, turned this down. 'Harming a diplomat is against the principle of diplomatic immunity', he emphasized.

The essence of diplomacy is negotiation with the overall objective of avoiding an unnecessary confrontation that may lead to challenges for both parties. In the process, it is important to try and understand the other person's perspectives and position and evaluate the mutual strengths and weaknesses of the parties involved.

At our workplace, it is important to be diplomatic with our bosses, peers, subordinates and other stakeholders. Diplomatic skills are a highly-valued skill for professionals across industries, as these skills improve workplace relationships and develop mutual respect among teammates, helping in eliminating workplace conflicts.

An illustrative example from our scriptures involves Lord Rama sending Angada to the court of Ravana with a message that Sita be returned safely to ensure that no further action would be taken by Lord Rama against Ravana. But the offer was declined.

Our scriptures include several such examples of diplomacy. Chanakya has written at length about diplomacy in *Arthashastra* and *Nitishastra*.

For Chanakya, diplomacy was very important. War, according to him, was the final option to attain a solution. Chanakya states that, for a nation, power is the means to attain stability and peace. Peace is achieved through careful manipulation of a nation's power.

Chanakya believed that diplomacy is a series of actions taken by a kingdom such that it gains strength and eventually conquers the nation with which diplomatic ties were created. He also believed that treaties should be made in such a way that the King benefits and serves the self-interest of the kingdom.

In Chanakya's Mandala theory, it is stated, 'Your neighbour is your natural enemy and the neighbour's neighbour is your friend.' *Mandala* is a Sanskrit word that means 'circles'.

Chanakya's Mandala theory and the six forms of diplomacy is a political model that helps to comprehend and address the complex structure of international relations and conflicts.

The Mandala theory propounds that in the circle of kings, a king's immediate neighbour is his enemy, while the neighbours of the enemy become allies. The circle expands to classify allies and adversaries, which aids the king in assessing relationships and forming strategies for alliances and warfare. To ensure the successful implementation of the Mandala theory, Chanakya proposed six forms of diplomacy: *Sandhi* (peace treaty), *Vigraha* (war), *Asana* (neutrality), *Yana* (military expedition), *Samsraya* (seeking shelter) and *Dvaidhibhava* (double policy).

1. *Sandhi* (peace treaty)

   In Sandhi, the king enters into a peace treaty with another king. The treaty ensures peaceful relations, allowing both kingdoms to grow and prosper without the fear of war. By making a pact with neighbouring kingdoms, kings can focus on internal development, strengthening their military and economic standing. This policy lays the groundwork for the successful execution of the Mandala theory by ensuring that the king has a secure and stable environment to execute further diplomatic and military strategies.

2. *Vigraha* (war)

   Vigraha entails the declaration of war against an adversary. Chanakya asserts that a king should go to war against a neighbouring king to expand his territory, weaken the enemy and strengthen his position. Vigraha is essential to the Mandala theory as it enables the king to neutralize immediate threats and establish dominance, ensuring his position and power in the Mandala.

3. *Asana* (neutrality)

   Asana involves maintaining a position of neutrality. When two neighbouring kingdoms are at war, the king adopts a neutral stance, waiting to align with the victor. This policy provides the king with the opportunity to conserve resources and analyse the evolving political landscape without getting directly involved. Asana is crucial in the Mandala theory, offering a strategic position that allows the king to make informed decisions based on the outcomes of conflicts among neighbours.

4. *Yana* (military expedition)

   Yana, or military expedition, is a proactive form of diplomacy. It entails the king leading a military expedition to expand his territory, establish dominance and showcase military might. Yana plays an essential role in the Mandala theory, ensuring the king's active involvement in shaping the geopolitical landscape, leading to the expansion and consolidation of his kingdom.

5. *Samsraya* (seeking shelter)

   In Samsraya, a weaker king seeks protection from a more powerful king against a common adversary. This policy fosters alliances, providing mutual benefits to both kingdoms. The weaker king receives protection, while the stronger king gains an ally, bolstering his position in the Mandala. Samsraya is vital in the Mandala theory, promoting cooperation and alliances essential for navigating the intricate dynamics of the geopolitical landscape.

6. *Dvaidhibhava* (double policy)
   Dvaidhibhava involves adopting a dual policy, involving both peace and hostility, with different kingdoms. It enables the king to maintain a balanced approach, keeping both allies and adversaries in check. The king can use peace treaties to stabilize relations with allies while engaging in hostile actions against enemies. Dvaidhibhava is indispensable to the Mandala theory, ensuring that the king can maintain a balanced and effective diplomatic approach.

These six forms of diplomacy can be used in various permutations and combinations depending upon the situation provided by the environment and must be used to gain the maximum benefit.

CHANAKYA'S UPAYAS

Upaya is a Sanskrit word that means an approach or an idea. Upaya also refers to the methods of diplomacy as practiced in our scriptures.

The four ideas or *Upayas* as outlined by Chanakya are *sama, dama, danda* and *bheda*. These are ways to reach a solution to avoid conflict. This phrase is also commonly used when we need to find a solution to a problem, one way or another.

1. *Sama*, the first step, means conciliation or alliance. When the situation of conflict arises, the first step is to talk.

2. *Dama*, the second step, means the price we may have to pay to resolve a conflict. Sometimes dama is also referred to as dana, meaning gifts or compensation.
3. *Danda* refers to force or coercion. This is only recommended as a last resort.
4. *Bheda* refers to the usage of logic or tricks to influence the mind.

All four ideas or *Upayas* are generally spoken together in a single colloquial phrase, 'Sama, Dama, Danda, Bheda'. This is a very common quote that is used all over India as a suggestion to resolve any conflict.

CHANAKYA'S LESSONS

Chanakya as well as our scriptures teach us the following:

There is no point in occupying the high moral ground if you lose in the process

Contemporary Indian politics is often saturated with an obsession over maintaining high moral ground, no matter the cost.

King Prithviraj Chauhan defeated and captured the Afghan Turk invader Muhammad Ghori. However, he released his prisoner as that was considered morally correct. Muhammad returned, defeated, captured and executed Prithviraj. This event led to Muslim rule over the entire Ganges river valley. Lord Krishna, in contrast, recommended the use of various strategies in the service of moral causes. The end justifies the means when major issues are at stake.

War is sometimes justified

The Hindu tradition has acquired a reputation for being exclusively non-violent. We say with pride that India has never attacked another country. While this is an interesting and noble viewpoint, war may sometimes be necessary, if only for self-defence.

Lord Krishna tells Arjuna on the battlefield that once a war breaks out, it is not only justifiable but mandatory to fight if it is for a good cause. It is also necessary to resort to war to bring about a desired conclusion rather than to walk away from violence out of the principle of non-violence.

Rules and customs can be interpreted flexibly

Context is a very important word in most of our scriptures. The *Mahabharata* states that rules and customs should be followed but they can be discarded or loosely followed should the need arise. Duty can therefore be amended if it pursues a course of action that is inflexible.

The Pandavas felt honour bound to play a game of dice a second time despite losing everything the first time and having their losses restored by Dhritarashtra. This notion of duty and honour may not always serve our needs and should be abandoned.

The *Mahabharata*, though an ancient epic, still has a lot to teach modern India. Its timeless lessons continue to guide Indian thinking. It argues that it's sometimes better to resort to what seems to be unjust in order to achieve greater justice.

CONVERSATION STARTERS

How often have we heard from our superiors at work that we must be more diplomatic? How often have we heard that our people skills are being watched and observed before we can be considered for a larger role in the organization?

Our capability to negotiate with others or interact with others will help us to stand apart. Tact and diplomacy are methods used to aid effective communication, especially during negotiation and when attempting to be persuasive or assertive.

The following can be considered when in conversation with another person:

1. When you're planning a potentially difficult conversation, think about the outcome you want and what you are trying to achieve. Once you have this clear, the path forward becomes straightforward. Separate your personal opinions that may introduce bias to your thinking during any such discussions.
2. Do not play dirty. Being diplomatic does not mean we have to cheat or lie. It is not about repackaging the truth to make someone or something 'look good'. Sticking to facts and being truthful is supremely important as trust is crucial to diplomacy.
3. Try to remain calm and keep an open mind. Find out the facts as well as what is and what is not possible before you react. When communicating, listen to what the other person has to say and try and understand the other person's point of view. Watch out for non-verbal communication and body language. Hold back your

response till you understand your own position.
4. Understand emotional intelligence. Inspire others to take action. Naming, blaming and shaming are not diplomatic actions. Help people understand your objectives through what they want and not what we want. Encourage people to talk about themselves and make them feel important.
5. A negotiation must be a win-win for both sides. Negotiation is a give-and-take process. There will always be a middle path that may satisfy everyone. Yet, we need to be assertive and firm and not be overly submissive.
6. Do not show your desperation, no matter how desperately you want to conclude a deal or get something. The harder we try, the needier we are and that has a direct bearing on our charisma. Just when the other person is expecting you to chase them to conclude a transaction, it is time to step back and make the other person think of the consequences if you were to walk away.

MANAGEMENT MANTRAS

Diplomacy is the art of negotiating and communicating with others to achieve a common goal or to resolve a conflict.

It is a critical skill that every manager should possess to achieve success in their careers. Diplomacy can help managers build relationships, handle difficult situations and make informed decisions that positively impact their organizations.

Diplomacy starts with effective communication

A manager should have excellent listening skills and be able to articulate their thoughts and ideas in a clear and concise manner. By being an active listener and showing empathy, a manager can gain the trust and respect of their employees, colleagues and partners. Communication is not only about exchanging information but also about understanding and finding common ground. When managers communicate effectively, they can build a culture of collaboration, trust and respect.

Diplomacy is the ability to negotiate

Managers are often faced with situations where they need to negotiate with suppliers, customers and employees. A good negotiator is able to find a mutually beneficial solution that meets the needs and goals of both parties. A diplomatic manager is able to identify the interests of each party and find a compromise that will benefit everyone. By building trust and understanding, a manager can create long-term relationships with their stakeholders.

Diplomacy is about handling difficult situations

Managers often encounter conflicts between employees, departments or stakeholders. Diplomatic managers are able to handle these conflicts in a professional and effective manner. They are able to assess the situation, listen to all parties involved and find a solution that is in the best interest of everyone. They are also able to mediate disputes in a way that is fair and equitable, and that protects the interests of their organization.

LEGACY

एवं प्रवर्तितं चक्रं नानुवर्तयतीह यः।
अघायुरिन्द्रियारामो मोघं पार्थ स जीवति।।

He who does not follow the wheel of creation
(i.e. does not perform his duties) and instead lives only
for the delight of his senses is sinful and lives in pain.

—*Bhagavad Gita, Chapter 3, Verse 16*

Hinduism places great importance on the concept of legacy. Our scriptures, including the Vedas, Upanishads and *Bhagavad Gita*, contain teachings and references to one of the key principles in Hinduism that every action has consequences, and these consequences can affect not only the individual who performed the action but also those who come after them. This idea is expressed through the concept of karma, which states that every action has a reaction and that this reaction will determine the individual's fate in future lives.

Another way that legacy is emphasized in our scriptures is through the idea of *dharma* or moral duty. Hindus believe that every individual has a specific dharma or purpose in life and that fulfilling this dharma will lead to a virtuous and fulfilling life. The performance of one's dharma is considered to be of the utmost importance as it can leave a positive impact on future generations.

In Hinduism, the idea of legacy is also tied to the concept of reincarnation. Hindus believe that the soul is immortal and that it reincarnates after death, moving from one life to the next. The legacy left behind in a previous life can shape the individual's future lives and experiences. Good deeds and actions can lead to a more positive and fulfilling life, while negative actions can result in hardship and suffering.

Our scriptures also emphasize the importance of leaving a spiritual legacy. Hindus believe that the ultimate goal of life is to attain *moksha* or liberation from the cycle of birth and death. By leading a virtuous and spiritual life, an individual can not only impact their own life positively but also leave behind a lasting spiritual legacy for future generations.

BHAGAVAD GITA ON LEGACY

Lord Krishna is revered for his wisdom, compassion and leadership. In the *Bhagavad Gita*, he outlines the concept of legacy and its importance for individuals and society as a whole.

He begins by emphasizing the importance of our actions and how they determine our legacy. He states that every action a person takes, good or bad, has a long-term impact on the world and our own soul. The law of karma dictates that the fruits of our actions will follow us into the next life. Thus, it is crucial for individuals to act with intention and responsibility, creating a legacy of positive impact.

Lord Krishna further emphasizes the importance of leaving a legacy that serves a higher purpose. He teaches that individuals should aim to fulfil their dharma and that their actions should align with their dharma. This creates a legacy that goes beyond the individual and serves the greater good of society and the universe.

Lord Krishna also highlights the power of legacy to shape future generations. He says that a virtuous legacy can inspire future generations to follow in the footsteps of the one who left it. In this way, a legacy can impact not just one's own life but also the lives of countless others in the future.

THE *RAMAYANA* ON LEGACY

Lord Rama, the seventh avatar of Lord Vishnu, is portrayed as a man with a strong character and unwavering principles, who always acted in accordance with dharma regardless of the circumstances. Throughout his life, Lord Rama upheld the values of truth, compassion and justice, and his legacy reflects these qualities.

For Lord Rama, legacy was not just about leaving behind a memorable name or an enduring impact, but about living a life that was in alignment with dharma. By following dharma, Lord Rama ensured that his actions would have a positive impact on society and future generations. This is why he is revered by Hindus as a role model and why his story continues to be retold even today.

In addition to his adherence to dharma, Lord Rama's legacy is also marked by his selflessness and devotion to his family and his kingdom. When his wife Sita was abducted by Ravana, Lord Rama did not hesitate to embark on a long and arduous journey to rescue her. Throughout the journey, he displayed courage, determination and a steadfast commitment to his duty, even in the face of great adversity.

Lord Rama's legacy is one of dharma, righteousness and selfless service. By living a life that was in alignment with these values, he left behind a lasting impact that continues to inspire people even today.

THE UPANISHADS ON LEGACY

The Upanishads discuss the concept of legacy as a crucial aspect of human existence. A legacy, in this context, is defined as a gift or bequest that is passed down from one generation to another and is often viewed as a reflection of one's life and values. In the Upanishads, legacy is seen as a means of transcending the boundaries of time and space and connecting to a universal, eternal reality.

One of the most prominent themes in the Upanishads is the idea of reincarnation. The legacy that a person leaves behind is seen as a reflection of their soul's journey through time and it is considered to be of great importance in determining the nature of the next life. This idea of legacy is closely tied to the concept of karma.

The Upanishads emphasize the importance of leaving behind a positive legacy, as it is believed that our actions in this life have a direct impact on our future existence. A person who lives a virtuous life, following the principles of truth, compassion and non-violence, is believed to leave behind a positive legacy that will guide them in their next life. In contrast, a person who lives an immoral life, engaging in acts of violence, deceit and cruelty, is believed to leave behind a negative legacy that will lead to their suffering in the next life.

In the Upanishads, legacy is not only limited to a person's physical existence but is also seen as a means of transcending the boundaries of time and space. The legacy of a person's life and actions is believed to continue beyond their death, influencing future generations.

This idea of legacy is closely tied to the concept of Atman, which is the individual soul that is seen as a part of the universal soul, Brahman.

CHANAKYA ON LEGACY

For Chanakya, legacy was an important aspect of a person's life that played a crucial role in shaping the future.

In Chanakya's view, a person's legacy was not simply a matter of what they left behind in terms of material wealth and possessions. Instead, he saw legacy as the impact that a person had on the world, both during their lifetime and after their death. For Chanakya, a person's legacy was a reflection of their character, values and beliefs, and it was this that would shape the future of society and the world.

One of Chanakya's most famous teachings on legacy was his emphasis on the importance of good deeds. He believed that a person's good deeds would always be remembered and would have a permanent effect on the world. He encouraged people to live their lives with integrity, wisdom and compassion so that they could leave behind a legacy that would inspire future generations.

Another important aspect of Chanakya's view on legacy was his emphasis on education. He believed that education was the key to shaping a person's legacy, as it was through education that people could develop their minds and gain the knowledge and skills needed to make a positive impact on the world. He believed that education should be accessible to all, regardless of social class or background, and that everyone should have the opportunity to learn and grow.

Chanakya also believed that legacy was not just about an individual but about the collective. He believed that every person had a role to play in shaping the world and that everyone's legacy was connected and interdependent. He encouraged people to work together and support one another in their efforts to create a better world so that the legacy of one generation could be passed on to the next.

MANAGEMENT MANTRAS

Legacy is a term that is often associated with history, heritage and inheritance.

In the context of management, legacy refers to the impact that a manager has on the organization, its people and its future. A manager's legacy can be thought of as the lasting impression that they leave behind, and the influence that they have on the organization long after they have left. This can be both positive and negative.

For example, a manager who is known for their innovative ideas and forward-thinking leadership style may be remembered for the positive changes that they brought about in the organization. In contrast, a manager who is known for their poor leadership skills and lack of concern for the well-being of employees may be remembered for the negative impact that they had on the organization.

To leave a positive legacy, managers need to be conscious of the impact that they are having on the organization and its people. They need to be mindful of their actions, words and decisions, and how these may impact the organization in the long run. This means taking the time to consider the consequences of their decisions and being amenable to make changes if necessary.

One way for managers to ensure that they are leaving

a positive legacy is by developing a strong leadership style that is focused on employee empowerment and engagement. This means creating an environment where employees feel valued, supported and encouraged to contribute their ideas and suggestions. By empowering employees, managers can help to build a culture of innovation and creativity, which can lead to positive changes and growth within the organization.

Another way for managers to leave a positive legacy is by investing in the development and growth of their employees. This means providing opportunities for employees to learn, grow and advance their careers within the organization. By helping employees reach their full potential, managers can help build a strong and talented workforce that is capable of driving the organization forward.

Managers can leave a positive legacy by being transparent and honest in their dealings with employees and stakeholders.

This means being open about the organization's goals and plans and engaging with employees and stakeholders to understand their needs and concerns. By building trust and creating a culture of transparency and honesty, managers can help ensure that the organization is well-positioned for success in the future.

MANAGEMENT CHAKRAS

The seven chakras, derived from ancient Indian spiritual tradition, represent the energy centres in the human body. These chakras are believed to govern various aspects of physical, emotional and mental wellness. The word 'chakra' in Sanskrit translates to 'wheel', symbolizing the continuous flow of energy.

Our life, especially our working life, can also be divided into seven chakras. Each 'life' chakra represents a critical aspect of work that we need to take care of in order to succeed.

I have attempted to draw life lessons from the energy centres of our body, including the crucial aspects needed for our success, in my book.

MULADHARA OR ROOT CHAKRA: LAYING THE FOUNDATION, CREATING SOMETHING NEW

Muladhara or the Root Chakra is the first of the seven primary chakras according to Hindu and Buddhist traditions. Located at the base of the spine, it forms the foundation of the entire chakra system, embodying stability, survival and security. Its balanced functioning is paramount for the free flow of energy (*Prana* or *Chi*) through the other chakras, laying a robust groundwork for overall well-being.

When embarking on creating something new, the root chakra plays a critical role. A balanced Muladhara provides the stability and security necessary to navigate the uncertainties and challenges of new ventures. It gives us the strength to stay grounded and centred amidst external fluctuations, allowing us to focus on our goals without succumbing to fear or doubt.

On the contrary, an imbalanced root chakra may manifest as anxiety, insecurity and lack of focus, thereby obstructing the path to creation and innovation. The nurturing energy of a balanced Muladhara Chakra fosters a resilient foundation necessary for any new endeavour. It allows us to stand firm in our intentions, ensuring a steady and sure path forward in the journey of creation. Engaging in practices that balance the root chakra, such as meditation, grounding exercises and working with grounding crystals and stones, is essential for laying a strong foundation for any new venture.

SVADHISHTHANA OR SACRAL CHAKRA: INVOKING SHAKTI, INFUSING ENERGY

The Svadhishthana or the Sacral Chakra governs creativity, sexual energy and emotional balance. It's associated with the water element, reflecting its fluidity and adaptability. A balanced Svadhishthana Chakra promotes emotional intelligence and creative expression and fortifies interpersonal relationships; when imbalanced, it can lead to emotional instability and lack of creativity. This chakra is positioned in the lower abdomen and is symbolized by an orange lotus with six petals.

Invoking Shakti pertains to the awakening of the divine feminine energy believed to reside within everyone. Shakti embodies the primal, cosmic energy, representing the dynamic forces that animate the universe. The act of invoking Shakti is to summon this universal power, catalysing spiritual awakening and enlightenment. It is about embracing the divine energy, permitting it to flow through the body, revitalizing and invigorating all dimensions of existence.

Whereas working with the Svadhishthana Chakra involves the specific aim of balance and emotional and creative harmony, invoking Shakti engages the broader, encompassing energy that pervades the universe. It may also stimulate and balance the Svadhishthana Chakra, among others, by infusing us with universal, vibrant energy. The intertwining of these concepts emphasizes the intricate balance and interplay between the specific energies of the chakras and the overarching cosmic energy of Shakti. Both contribute to our holistic well-being, empowerment and spiritual advancement.

MANIPURA OR SOLAR PLEXUS CHAKRA: COURAGE AND MENTAL RESOLVE

The Manipura or the Solar Plexus Chakra is the third primary chakra according to Vedic tradition, positioned at the solar plexus area. It is the core of our personality, identity and ego, symbolized by a bright yellow colour and represented by a ten-petal lotus flower. It is the centre of willpower and self-discipline. In Sanskrit, '*Manipura*' means 'lustrous gem', reflecting its potent qualities.

The impact of the Manipura Chakra on courage and

mental resolve is profound. It is considered the seat of personal power and autonomy, and a balanced Manipura Chakra reflects in the form of confidence, clarity and the ability to take decisive action. It empowers us to follow through with their convictions, reinforcing courage and inner strength. It strengthens mental resolve, enabling us to overcome obstacles, face fears and work towards our goals with determination and perseverance.

An unbalanced Manipura Chakra may result in feelings of powerlessness, fear and anxiety, which undermine courage and mental resolve. We may find it hard to take action, make decisions or assert ourselves, leading to feelings of inadequacy and insecurity. Balancing this chakra through various spiritual practices, including meditation, yoga and breathwork, can help restore confidence, courage and mental fortitude, enabling us to navigate life's challenges with resilience and assurance.

ANAHATA OR HEART CHAKRA: EMOTIONAL INTELLIGENCE AND ACCOUNTABILITY

The Anahata or the Heart Chakra, located at the centre of the chest, is the focal point for love, compassion and spirituality. This chakra, associated with the air element, governs relationships and emotional balance. A harmonious Anahata Chakra encourages love, empathy and forgiveness; when imbalanced, it can lead to emotional turmoil and challenges in relationships.

This chakra is the fourth primary chakra in the body's subtle energy system, traditionally located at the centre of the chest. It's seen as the epicentre of love, compassion and empathy, deeply intertwined with emotional intelligence and accountability. Emotional intelligence involves recognizing, understanding and managing our own emotions and the emotions of others. When the Anahata Chakra is balanced, it aids in this by fostering self-awareness and compassion, allowing us to connect with others on a profound level.

It encourages emotional responsiveness and vulnerability, paving the way for honest and open interactions. In terms of accountability, a balanced Anahata Chakra enables us to take responsibility for our actions and emotions, promoting personal integrity. It assists in the cultivation of a strong moral compass, guiding us to act ethically and empathetically. Through the harmonization of the Anahata Chakra, we are better equipped to navigate our emotional landscapes, foster meaningful relationships and embody accountability in all aspects of our lives.

VISHUDDHI OR THROAT CHAKRA: CONNECTING THE DOTS WITH STAKEHOLDERS

The Vishuddhi or the Throat Chakra holds immense significance in ensuring effective communication and establishing robust connections with stakeholders in various aspects of life and work. Located at the throat, this fifth energy centre is associated with communication, expression and the ability to speak one's truth clearly.

In business and organizational contexts, the harmonious functioning of this chakra can be integral to connecting the dots with stakeholders. An open and balanced Vishuddhi enables us to express our thoughts, ideas and emotions transparently, fostering an environment of mutual respect, understanding and collaboration. It encourages active listening, a crucial aspect of stakeholder engagement, allowing for the absorption of diverse perspectives and insights. This receptivity enhances decision-making and problem-solving capabilities, ensuring that the needs and concerns of all stakeholders are considered.

Moreover, an aligned Vishuddhi Chakra helps in navigating difficult conversations with grace, addressing conflicts constructively and ensuring that communication is respectful and empathetic. It aids in articulating visions, goals and strategies effectively, ensuring that all stakeholders are on the same page, contributing positively to the realization of shared objectives. In essence, the throat chakra's equilibrium plays a pivotal role in strengthening relationships with stakeholders, leading to more cohesive, inclusive and successful collaborations.

AJNA OR THIRD-EYE CHAKRA: HOLISTIC COMMUNICATION AND AWARENESS

The Ajna or the Third-Eye Chakra is the sixth energy centre located in the forehead, slightly above the space between the eyebrows. It is considered the epicentre of intuition, insight and inner wisdom, playing a pivotal role in holistic communication and awareness.

Holistic communication extends beyond verbal or written exchanges. It encompasses a deeper level of connectivity and understanding with ourselves and others, transcending the barriers of language and perception. The Ajna Chakra's harmonious operation significantly influences this form of communication. An activated third-eye chakra enables individuals to access enhanced levels of consciousness and awareness, aligning them with their innermost thoughts, feelings and intuitions. This alignment helps in understanding the unsaid, perceived energies, and the underlying essence of interpersonal exchanges, leading to more empathetic and compassionate interactions.

Moreover, the Ajna Chakra's influence on awareness is paramount. It awakens our ability to see beyond the physical realm, tapping into higher realms of perception and consciousness. This expanded awareness allows for a heightened sensitivity to external environments, fostering a more harmonious existence and connection with the universe and all living beings within it. When balanced, the third-eye chakra enables us to effectively navigate our lives with intuition and insight, contributing to effective communication and a profound understanding of the interconnectedness of all things.

SAHASRARA OR CROWN CHAKRA: CONNECTING BUSINESSES WITH THE PEOPLE

The Sahasrara or the Crown Chakra is the seventh chakra, symbolizing the state of pure consciousness. Situated at the crown of the head, it is considered the gateway to the universal consciousness, where individual awareness merges with the infinite. It's believed to govern spiritual insight, enlightenment and the connection with the Divine.

The Sahasrara Chakra can be seen as a unifying force transcending boundaries. It echoes the essence of universal interconnectedness and oneness, illuminating the understanding that every being is interconnected in the grand tapestry of existence. This principle of unity and oneness provides a solid foundation for establishing harmony and balance in the world, which is essential for the mutual growth and prosperity of businesses and communities.

In connecting businesses with the people, the Sahasrara Chakra's emphasis on universal consciousness can guide organizations to adopt a more inclusive, sustainable and humane approach. It promotes the recognition of the interconnectedness of all elements of the business ecosystem, including the communities they serve, fostering a mutualistic relationship. By embodying the principles associated with the crown chakra, businesses can better understand and respond to the needs and aspirations of communities, facilitating not only their own growth and stability but also contributing meaningfully to global well-being and progress.

In conclusion, the seven chakras are fundamental aspects of understanding holistic well-being from a spiritual perspective. Balancing these chakras through various methods such as meditation, yoga and other healing practices is believed to provide physical, emotional and mental harmony, promoting overall well-being and a deeper connection with the self and the universe. Understanding the specific attributes, locations and elements associated with each chakra allows us to focus on areas in our lives that may require attention and healing, fostering growth, balance and spiritual development.

Similarly, it is important to balance the chakras in both professional and personal spheres, as a balanced life will yield significant results.

Part Two

Wisdom from Indic Scriptures

THE VEDAS

The term *Veda* means knowledge, derived from the Sanskrit word 'vid'.

The Vedas are considered among the oldest works in Sanskrit literature as well as the oldest scriptures of Hinduism. Vedic culture is the indigenous culture of India: it is not merely a code of religion but a way of life, regardless of what level of consciousness or inquiry into spiritual truths that a person may have.

The Vedas are directed towards one goal, which is to achieve the union of the individual self or *Atman* with the world self or *Brahman*.

Vedic wisdom pays a great deal of attention to the transformation of the inner self. The purpose of this is not so much external effectiveness as it is to connect with a higher self. It is about the awakening of a higher understanding of our human aspiration and in simple terms about an understanding of who we are.

Of all the many sacred texts, Hindus accord supernatural origin only to the Vedas. The Vedas are trusted to reveal the essential knowledge of life. Such knowledge has existed eternally in the form of vibrations sounding throughout the universe. These vibrations remained undetected until certain

Indian sages equipped with spiritual hearing finally heard and formulated them in the Sanskrit language.

No one knows the origin of the Vedas although many scholars and theologians have presented differing claims on the subject. The Vedic age began when the Sanskrit-speaking people began to dominate life and thought in the Indus Valley, probably between 2000 and 1500 BCE. The Vedas are thought to reproduce the exact sounds of the universe itself at the moment of creation and onwards and so take the form of hymns and chants. In reciting the Vedas, one is thought to be literally participating in the creative song of the universe that gave birth to all things from the beginning of time.

The Vedas existed in oral form and were passed down from master to student for generations until they were committed to writing between 1500 and 900 BCE, which is also referred to as the Vedic period in India. The teachings were carefully preserved orally. The masters would make students memorize them forward and backward with emphasis on exact pronunciation to keep what was originally heard intact.

The Saptarshis have played a significant role in contributing their knowledge and revelations to the Vedas. There are four Vedas. We will discuss these briefly.

- *Rig Veda*
- *Sama Veda*
- *Yajur Veda*
- *Atharva Veda*

Each of these is further divided into types of text included within them:

- Aranyakas: rituals, observances
- Brahmanas: commentaries on the rituals
- Samhitas: benedictions, prayers and mantras
- Upanishads: philosophical narratives and dialogues

Maharishi Vedavyasa, considered to be one of the greatest acharyas of sanatana dharma, was responsible for classifying the four Vedas. Vedavyasa literally means 'the splitter of Vedas'. It is believed that this division of the Vedas into four parts made it easy for people to read and understand the scriptures better. He wrote the 18 Puranas and recited the *Mahabharata*, often referred to as the fifth Veda. The life of Vedavyasa is an example of how to be selfless and devote oneself entirely to the Lord to attain nirvana.

RIG VEDA

The *Rig Veda* stands as the oldest among the Vedas, comprising 1,028 hymns with approximately 10,600 verses. These verses speak about proper religious observance and practice based on the universal vibrations as understood by the Rishis who first heard them.

Vedic thinkers asked questions about how, what and why. They asked about themselves, the world around them and the place each one of us occupies in it. They would ask questions like what is thought, why the wind blows, who put the sun in the sky, how the world has so many life forms, etc. The *Rig Veda* encourages these kinds of questions through hymns in the praise of the *Devatas*.

This reflection characterizes the essence of Hinduism in that the point of personal existence is to question it as one moves from the basic needs of life towards self-actualization and union with the Divine.

SAMA VEDA

The *Sama Veda* is a work of songs, chants and texts meant to be sung. The content is almost wholly derived from the *Rig Veda*, which serves as the lyrics to the melodies contained in the *Sama Veda*. It has 1,875 verses. The melodies are believed to encourage dance that, combined with the words, elevates the soul.

YAJUR VEDA

The *Yajur Veda* derives its name from the root word 'yaj', which means worship. It consists of recitations, ritual worship formulas, mantras and chants directly involved in worship services. It has 1,975 verses on religious practices and observances.

ATHARVA VEDA

The *Atharva Veda* differs significantly from the first three. It contains chants, hymns, prayers, initiation rituals, marriage and funeral ceremonies, observations on daily life and spells to ward off evil spirits or danger. It has 730 hymns with about 6,000 verses.

THE VEDAS AND MODERN MANAGEMENT

The roots of human motivation lie in cultural values. An understanding of our scriptures is therefore an important aspect of being able to manage across cultures. Most management philosophies draw upon the teachings of our scriptures.

The Vedic path consists of 10 general rules of moral conduct. There are five rules each of conduct for internal purity (*Yamas*) and external purity (*Niyamas*), as follows:

Yamas

1. *Satya* or truthfulness
2. *Ahimsa* or non-violence and treating all beings with respect
3. *Asteya* or no cheating or stealing
4. *Brahmacharya* or celibacy
5. *Aparigraha* or no selfish accumulation of resources for our own purpose

Niyamas

1. *Shaucha* or cleanliness and purity of mind and body
2. *Tapas* or austerity and perseverance
3. *Svadhyaya* or study of the Vedas
4. *Santosh* or contentment
5. *Ishvara* or acceptance of the Supreme

In addition to the Yamas and Niyams, there are 10 qualities that are the basis of dharmic (righteous) life. These are:

1. *Dhriti* or firmness or fortitude
2. *Kshma* or forgiveness
3. *Dama* or self-control
4. *Asteya* or refraining from stealing or dishonesty
5. *Shauch* or purity
6. *Indriya nigraha* or control over the senses

7. *Dhih* or intellect
8. *Vidya* or knowledge
9. *Satyam* or truth
10. *Akrodhah* or absence of anger

We have five obligatory duties or responsibilities as humans. These include:

1. *Brahma-yajna* or service to the sages
2. *Deva-yajna* or service to the Gods
3. *Pitr-yajna* or service to your parents and ancestors
4. *Manushya-yajna* or service to fellow human beings
5. *Bhuta-yajna* or service to the rest of the creatures

Vedic wisdom acknowledges that everyone is unique, and everyone has their own path to follow. It describes four *ashramas* or stages in life.

1. The Brahmacharya or student phase
2. The Grihastha or householder phase
3. The Vanaprastha or preparation for renunciation phase
4. The Sanyasa or renunciation phase

For centuries, the Vedas have been the fountainhead of all knowledge for us. Our scriptures have always been pragmatic, and our spiritual leaders have interpreted these scriptures in the current context. This interpretation enables every subsequent generation to accept these scriptures based on their understanding and context.

Let us look at four such verses relating to wealth in *Rig Veda*. These generally invoke Gods and Goddesses for blessings of prosperity, well-being and protection from enemies and misfortune. These are an adaptation and not a direct translation from the Rig Veda:

> O Agni, the giver of Life, bless us with affluence.
> Shower upon us the riches of the bounteous earth.
> May we find wealth in your warmth and light,
> And walk the path of prosperity, bright and clear.
>
> Indra, the mighty, with your thunderous power,
> Bestow upon us the strength to acquire wealth.
> May our lands be fertile, and our herds multiply,
> Grant us the courage and vigour in life's battles.
>
> O Saraswati, in your flowing grace we seek,
> The wisdom to create and share abundant wealth.
> Bless our minds with insight and our hands with skill,
> To nurture prosperity in harmony with the cosmos.
>
> O Varuna, keeper of cosmic order,
> May our endeavours align with the laws of the universe.
> Grant us the discernment to act justly and wisely,
> Ensuring our wealth is a force for good and light.

The *Rig Veda* advocates the need to conserve our resources for future needs. We are aware of the need to save for the future. Creation of wealth is seen as a positive and removal of poverty is seen as a necessity for society. Future necessities must never be compromised for short-term goals or desires.

GAYATRI MANTRA

ॐ भूर्भुवः स्वः
तत्सवितुर्वरेण्यं
भर्गो देवस्य धीमहि।
धियो यो नः प्रचोदयात्।।

Om bhūr bhuvaḥ svaḥ
tatsaviturvareaṇyaṃ
bhargo devasyadhīmahi
dhiyo yo naḥ prachodayāt

—*Rig Veda, Book 3, Chapter 62, Verse 10*

The Gayatri mantra was believed to be first recorded in the *Rig Veda* and was written in Sanskrit. Rishi Vishvamitra is believed to be the creator of the Gayatri Mantra. This mantra is a hymn for the Sun God where the sun represents the actual sun as well as the Divine present in all beings. Just as the sun illuminates the land, this mantra is believed to fill the person chanting it with all the potential energy in the cosmos. The Gayatri mantra calls upon the infinite light of consciousness to guide our actions and beliefs. It is possibly the most widely chanted verse from any scripture anywhere in the world.

The Gayatri mantra comprises 24 syllables organized inside a triplet of eight syllables. It is considered one of the most universal of all mantras, invoking the universal Brahman as the principle of knowledge and the illumination of the primordial sun.

Goddess Gayatri represents infinite knowledge. It is she who eliminates the darkness or ignorance from our lives and helps us attain enlightenment by showering us with the wisdom that we need in our day-to-day life as well as the life beyond.

The words of the Gayatri mantra can be interpreted as 'O thou existence Absolute, Creator of the three dimensions, we contemplate upon thy divine light. May He stimulate our intellect and bestow upon us true knowledge.'

It can also be read to mean 'O Divine Mother, our hearts are filled with darkness. Please make this darkness distant from us and promote illumination within us.'

Twenty-six Gods have been named in the Gayatri mantra[*]:

Tat	*Ganesh*
Sa	*Narasimha*
Vi	*Vishnu*
Tu	*Shiva*
Va	*Krishna*
Re	*Radha*
Ni	*Lakshmi*
Yam	*Agni*
Bha	*Indra*
Rgo	*Saraswati*
De	*Durga*
Va	*Hanuman*
Sya	*Prithvi*
Dhee	*Surya*
Ma	*Ram*
Hi	*Sita*

---

[*]Rajan K, '26 Gods Mentioned in Gayatri Mantra', 6 June 2018, *Speakingtree. in*, Times Internet Limited, https://www.speakingtree.in/blog/26-gods-mentioned-in-gayatri-mantra.

Dhi	*Chandra*
Yo	*Yama*
Ya	*Brahma*
Na	*Varuna*
Pr	*Lakshmi and Vishnu*
Cho	*Hayagreeva*
Da	*Hamsa*
Yaat	*Tulasi*

It is believed that the repetitive chant or sound of the Gayatri mantra can focus our mind, elevate our consciousness through specific vibrations or frequencies and calm our nervous system.

I was taught by my mother to chant the Gayatri mantra and the Hanuman Chalisa whenever I was faced with any stress. I have chanted it repeatedly whenever my aircraft has hit turbulence or when I am faced with a challenging situation. For me, this is no magic. Repeated chanting of the Gayatri mantra helps me to calm my mind; when my mind is calm, I am able to think clearly without panicking.

The Gayatri mantra has taught me the following lessons:

1. *Give back to the sun:* It is accepted that the sun always gives and never receives anything in return. Chanting the Gayatri mantra is our way of expressing our gratitude to the life-giving sun and the Divine.
2. *Seek wisdom and enlightenment:* The Gayatri mantra is a request to the sun asking it if we as human beings may meditate upon the form of the sun that gives its energy and illumination without any attachment or outcome.

Think of all the opportunities we have in our daily lives at work and home, in societies we live in and with the people who cross our paths every day. Think of how often we are able to express our gratitude or thank them for simply being a part of our lives. If someone has given us something, then this gratitude and acknowledgement becomes even more important and relevant.

In conclusion, the Vedic texts contain a wealth of meaning. One needs to understand the words carefully and then apply the context of these words to our lives and the situations we are faced with.

Besides its poetic grandeur these texts contain detailed narratives for order in society and social life, great philosophical truths as well as scientific laws. The Vedic management concepts curated in ancient times are relevant even today.

The knowledge and wisdom in the Vedas show the righteous path to the entrepreneurs of the modern world.

The Vedas form the foundational understanding of Sanatana Dharma and provide a direction and purpose in the lives of believers. The Brahman not only created existence but was existence itself. As this entity was too great to be comprehended by human beings, he appeared as avatars such as Brahma, the creator; Vishnu, the preserver; and Shiva, the destroyer. In addition, there may be several deities but all of them are actually the Brahman.

The purpose of human life is to recognize our higher self, the *Atman* and perform the dharma or duty one has been given with the proper karma or action to free ourselves from the cycle of rebirth and death. Once an individual has broken these bonds the Atman returns to Brahman and eternal peace.

THE BHAGAVAD GITA

चञ्चलं हि मनः कृष्ण प्रमाथि बलवद्दृढम्।
तस्याहं निग्रहं मन्ये वायोरिव सुदुष्करम्॥

The mind is restless, obstinate and strong, O Krishna.
It is more difficult to control the mind
than it is to control the wind.

—*Bhagavad Gita, Chapter 6, Verse 34*

As managers, our objective is to become better leaders and learn the art of effective delegation. We need to motivate our teams and encourage our workforce. We must ensure accountability and commitment at our place of work.

The critical question in the mind of every manager is how to be effective in their job, enabling them to move ahead in their careers. The answer to this fundamental question is present in the *Bhagavad Gita*, which repeatedly states that each one of us must learn to manage ourselves. Unless we reach a certain level of excellence and effectiveness, we will not be able to differentiate ourselves.

Lord Krishna could rightfully be called the first coach in the world as he speaks to Arjuna on the battlefield.

Modern management deals with problems at material or peripheral levels. However, the *Gita* addresses these issues on the assumption that once our thoughts are clear, our actions and performance will improve. From a quarter-by-quarter approach where every leader is rushing to 'show' improved performance over the previous quarter or year, the *Gita* asks us to look at the fundamentals of our life and act accordingly instead of reacting to a particular event or transaction.

The philosophy of the *Gita* should not be viewed only from a devotional or religious perspective. It has a number of points that we can draw upon to develop our managerial effectiveness as well.

There is a moral dimension to our professional lives. What we do in our professional sphere is no different from what we do in our personal lives. The means do not justify the ends. The pursuit of results for their own sake is ultimately self-defeating.

We are drawing upon these verses and relating them to our lives. Every verse has been discussed and debated by thinkers and philosophers over the ages. There have been agreements and disagreements on the message that Krishna is conveying. We could have different interpretations that apply to our context and situation.

LESSONS FROM THE GITA

Leadership

Leadership is a critical management skill. Teams look towards managers to provide the direction and motivation to complete the work.

बलं बलवतां चाहं कामरागविवर्जितम्।
धर्माविरुद्धो भूतेषु कामोऽस्मि भरतर्षभ।।

—*Bhagavad Gita, Chapter 7, Verse 11*

Krishna says, 'I am the strength of those who are devoid of personal desire and attachment. O Arjuna, I am the legitimate desire in those who are not opposed to righteousness.'

The message is clear; the leader needs to believe in excellence for himself and this can be achieved by doing his work with commitment and sincerity.

Motivation

Motivation can be intrinsic or extrinsic.

Intrinsic motivation is driven by an interest or enjoyment in the task itself and exists within the individual rather than relying on any external pressure. Extrinsic motivation comes from outside of the individual. Examples of extrinsic motivation can be positive, such as money, or negative, such as coercion and threat of punishment.

कर्मण्येवाधिकारस्ते मा फलेषु कदाचन।
मा कर्मफलहेतुर्भूर्मा ते सङ्गोऽस्त्वकर्मणि।।

—*Bhagavad Gita, Chapter 2, Verse 47*

The *Gita* says, 'You certainly have a right to prescribed activities, but never at any time to their results. You should never be motivated by the results of the actions, nor there should be any attachment in not doing your prescribed activities.'

Decision-making

Making a decision is a choice.

The 18 chapters and 700 verses of the *Gita* have one objective: to ensure that Arjuna decides to pick up his *Gandiva* (his divine bow) and fight the Kurukshetra War. Krishna takes Arjuna through a voyage of self-discovery so that he can make the decision when he is faced with conflicting values.

Stick to the Goal Unwaveringly

The Pandavas were undergoing their training at the ashram of Guru Dronacharya.

One day, Dronacharya tied a wooden fish to a tree branch over some water. The Guru asked the brothers to aim for the eye of the fish but only by looking at the reflection of the fish in the water. Yudhishthira went first and when asked what he saw, he said he saw the sky, birds and the fish. Next Dronacharya asked Bhima who said he saw the tree, branches, leaves and the fish. Finally, Dronacharya asked Arjuna to take his position and asked him what he saw.

Arjuna responded that he saw the eye of the fish.

Commitment to Work

The *Gita* advises detachment from the fruits or results of actions performed in the course of our duty. It is important to detach from the rewards that may or may not follow.

If the result of our effort is a success, the entire credit should not be appropriated by the doer alone. If the result of our effort is a failure, then the entire blame must not fall only on the doer.

Utilization of Available Resources

One of the lessons of modern management is to use the available resources wisely.

At the start of the Kurukshetra War, Arjuna is filled with moral confusion and despair about fighting in the war, which involves killing his own relatives, revered elders and friends. Overwhelmed by sorrow and compassion, he contemplates abandoning the battlefield.

It is in this context that Lord Krishna imparts his divine wisdom to Arjuna. One of the many teachings Krishna provides pertains to the concept of '*Svadharma*' or one's own duty.

The concept of *Svadharma* can be interpreted as effectively using the resources and skills available to one. Arjuna, being a trained and skilled warrior, has a duty to use his abilities for the greater good. Avoiding the war would mean he's not putting his skills to the best use.

By extension, the *Gita* teaches that each of us, regardless of our role or station in life, has a set of skills and resources at our disposal. It becomes our duty, our *dharma*, to utilize those resources to the best of our ability for the benefit of ourselves and society.

In a broader context, not only does the *Gita* emphasize the importance of using one's personal skills and talents, but it also underscores the significance of using available physical and material resources wisely.

Practise what you Preach

Krishna says, 'Whatever the excellent and best ones do, the commoners follow.'

यद्यदाचरति श्रेष्ठस्तत्तदेवेतरो जनः।
स यत्प्रमाणं कुरुते लोकस्तदनुवर्तते॥

—*Bhagavad Gita, Chapter 3, Verse 21*

This verse emphasizes the need for leaders to act righteously, morally and wisely, as their actions directly mould the character and actions of their followers and society at large. It suggests a moral duty for those in leadership roles to maintain high standards of conduct and integrity, to guide others on the path of *dharma* or righteous living.

When leaders demonstrate positive and upright behaviour, it creates a ripple effect, encouraging similar behaviours and attitudes among their followers and contributing to the welfare and progress of society as a whole.

While leaders play a crucial role in setting examples for others to follow, followers also play a significant role by choosing whom to emulate. In an age characterized by diverse leadership styles and philosophies, this verse emphasizes the need for modern leaders to embody virtues such as humility, wisdom and integrity to pave the way for a harmonious and prosperous society.

Work Culture

One of the central teachings of the *Gita* is the importance of performing one's duty with commitment and sincerity. In a work context, this translates to fulfilling responsibilities with integrity, professionalism and a high standard of ethics. An organization that prioritizes these values nurtures a culture of trust, accountability and mutual respect among its employees. This, in turn, contributes to the organization's credibility, reputation and long-term success.

The *Gita* also provides guidance on maintaining equanimity in success and failure. It encourages individuals to remain balanced in all circumstances, avoiding excessive elation in success or despair in failure. By promoting this balanced mindset in the work culture, organizations can ensure that employees remain motivated, resilient and focused, irrespective of the external circumstances. This mental stability is crucial for maintaining productivity and positivity in the workplace, allowing employees to navigate challenges with grace and wisdom.

The *Gita's* philosophy promotes harmony and unity, emphasizing the interconnectedness of all beings. In a work environment, this philosophy encourages a culture of teamwork, mutual respect and inclusivity. Employees are motivated to collaborate, share knowledge and work towards the common goals of the organization, fostering a sense of unity and shared purpose. This interconnectedness enhances the organization's ability to innovate, adapt and thrive in a dynamic business landscape.

Steadiness of Mind and Motivation

Motivation plays a critical role in achieving goals and business objectives.

The *Bhagavad Gita* offers invaluable insights into the development of a steady mind and true motivation. By advocating detachment, focus on dharma and selfless action, the *Gita* provides a blueprint for personal and spiritual growth, leading to inner peace, fulfilment and ultimate liberation.

In the *Gita*, *sthita-prajna* or steadiness of mind is depicted as a state of inner equilibrium, a balance where the mind remains unwavering in the face of the world's dualities such as joy and sorrow, success and failure, honour and dishonour. A steady mind is clear, focused and unperturbed by external circumstances, embodying a deep inner peace and stability.

Motivation in the *Gita* is intertwined with the concept of dharma, or righteous duty.

Anger Management

When we are young, we tend to get angry more often when we see people not agreeing with the way we would like the work to be done. We know that anger harms no one other than ourselves. Yet we find it difficult to control and manage our emotional outbursts. As we get older, most of us mature and calm down though some continue to be challenged with the debilitating effects of anger.

Modern psychoanalysis suggests that anger is a manifestation of repressed and suppressed desires within us.

ध्यायतो विषयान्पुंसः सङ्गस्तेषूपजायते।
सङ्गात्सञ्जायते कामः कामात्क्रोधोऽभिजायते।।

—*Bhagavad Gita, Chapter 2, Verse 62*

Krishna says, 'desire for sense objects comes from attachment to them, and anger comes from unfulfilled desires.'

Mental Strength

Mental strength and sound health are the mutual goals of every human being. We either aspire to always have a calm and positive state of mind or regain that state when unsettled in the midst of all external vagaries of work life and social existence. Internal peace is a prerequisite for a healthy, stress-free mind.

Some of the impediments to sound mental health are:

- Greed—for power, position, prestige and money
- Envy—regarding others' achievements, success and rewards
- Ego—about one's accomplishments
- Suspicion, anger and frustration

Krishna, in his conversation with Arjuna, addresses the need for mental strength in several verses of the *Gita*.

Commitment to Work

Most of us have been taught the importance of working with full dedication and commitment. We also have often been told that we must not look for a quid pro quo or a reward at work. We must do our best and the results will follow. The *Gita* advises 'detachment' from the fruits or results of actions performed in the course of our duty.

Yet, we experience disappointment when we do not get what we want in return for the work we believe we are doing. Working only with an eye on the expected return could result in a decreased quality of performance in the current job. The *Gita* tells us not to compromise our current commitment at work in the hope of a future that may not be there for us.

The *Gita* also mentions cause and effect, making us responsible for the consequences of our deeds. However, while the *Gita* advises detachment, it does not absolve us from the consequences arising from the discharge of our responsibilities.

The best example of our commitment is the work itself.

The contribution of the *Gita* in addition to spiritual knowledge also helps to understand the art of self-determination, our personality, behaviour, time management, stress management and many other aspects of management that can be used as a guide to increase management effectiveness.

THE RAMAYANA

> He came to India as Krishna, Rama and Buddha,
> and He will come again.
> It can almost be demonstrated that
> after every 500 years the world sinks,
> and a tremendous spiritual wave comes,
> on top of which is Christ.[*]
>
> —*Swami Vivekananda*

The *Ramayana* is one of the most widely read and understood Hindu scriptures. It is popular throughout South-East Asia.

The *Ramayana* was written by Rishi Valmiki. Its narrative is believed to have taken place during a period known as the Treta Yuga. According to Robert P. Goldman, the oldest parts of the *Ramayana* date to the mid-eighth century BCE.[**]

There are believed to be over 300 interpretations of the *Ramayana* spread over numerous Asian nations, including

---

[*]VivekaVani, 'Notes of Class Talks—Swami Vivekananda', 30 August 2011, https://vivekavani.com/notes-class-talks-swami-vivekananda-2/.
[**]Singh, Upinder, *Political Violence in Ancient India*, Harvard University Press, Cambridge, MA, 20 October 2017.

Thailand, Vietnam, Myanmar, Indonesia, Cambodia, Lao, Philippines and China. Interpretations also exist in various languages, some of which are as follows[*]:

1. The Tamil version is known as *Ramavataram*
2. The Telugu version is known as *Ranganatha Ramayana*
3. The Khmer version is known as *Reamker*
4. The Javanese version is known as *the Kakawin Ramayana*
5. The Pāli version is known as *Dasaratha Jataka*
6. The Prakrit version is known as *Paumachariya*
7. The Malay version is known as *Hikayat Seri Rama*
8. The Thai version is known as *Ramakien*
9. The Burmese version is known as *Yama Zatdaw*
10. The Lao version is known as *Phra Lak Phra Ram*
11. The Assamese version is known as *Saptakanda Ramayana*
12. The Malayalam version is known as *Ramacharitam*
13. Tulsidas' version, the most famous, is known as *Ramcharitmanas*

I have referred to *Valmiki's Ramayana* for this book, which has 24,000 verses divided into the following 7 *Kandas* (sections):

1. *Bala Kanda* describes Rama's birth, childhood and marriage to Sita.

---

[*]'The Ramayana's Different Versions', *Amar Chitra Katha*, 23 April 2020, https://www.amarchitrakatha.com/mythologies/the-ramayanas-different-versions/ and Pandhare, Mandar, '5 Surprising Ways in Which the Story of the Epic Ramayana Differs in Other Parts of Asia', *The Better India*, 26 June 2016, https://www.thebetterindia.com/58547/ramayana-story-different-asia-buddhist-jain-malaysia-thailand-burma/.

2. *Ayodhya Kanda* describes Rama's preparations for the coronation and his exile for 14 years.
3. *Aranya Kanda* describes the story of Rama's life in Panchavati, the story of Sita's abduction by Ravana and Jatayu's efforts to save her.
4. *Kishkindha Kanda* describes the reunion of Hanuman and Rama, killing of the monkey king Bali with Rama's help and coronation of Sugriva, Bali's younger brother, in the monkey kingdom of Kishkindha.
5. *Sundara Kanda* is the central part of the *Valmiki Ramayana*. This section deals with the detailed and explicit account of Hanuman's expedition and arrival in Lanka, his meeting with Sita and Hanuman's efforts to rescue Sita.
6. *Yuddha Kanda* describes the details of the battle of Rama and Ravana and the construction of Rama Setu.
7. *Uttara Kanda* describes the birth of Luv and Kush, their coronation and Rama's departure from the Earth.

LESSONS FROM THE RAMAYANA

Management Lessons

The *Ramayana* is an eternal source of guidance on how to live life in a manner that benefits society. Further, never commit any act that you will live to regret later. The actions of Lord Rama, his brothers (Bharata, Lakshmana and Shatrughna), Hanuman, Sita and other individuals leave an indelible mark on our minds.

Respect your Enemy

Ravana was defeated in the war by Rama after the former's brother Vibhishana told him that the only way to kill Ravana was to dry up the *amrita* (the nectar of eternal life) stored in his belly button. Thus, one arrow shot at Ravana's belly button led to his falling.

Rishi Valmiki has described Ravana as the greatest devotee of Shiva and a very learned individual. His ten heads represented *kama* (lust), *krodha* (anger), *moha* (delusion), *lobha* (greed), *mada* (pride), *matsarya* (envy), *manas* (mind), *buddhi* (intellect), *chitta* (will) and *ahamkara* (the ego).

As he lay on his deathbed on the battlefield, Rama asked Lakshmana to go to Ravana and take lessons from him as Ravana was a very knowledgeable person.

Lakshmana took the advice of his brother Rama and went to Ravana. He stood next to Ravana's head. Ravana told Lakshmana to stand near his feet if he had come as a student to learn something. After Lakshmana moved towards Ravana's feet, he gave him the following lessons:

a. *Value time*: Do not delay completing any auspicious work. Ravana said he failed to recognize Rama, and this delayed his achieving *moksha*.

b. *Never underestimate anyone*: Ravana said that he had underestimated and laughed at an army of monkeys and bears. He assumed that they would not be able to match his powerful demon army. This led to his defeat and the destruction of his army.

c. *Never reveal your secrets*: Ravana knew that his death had been caused because his brother (who was privy to Ravana's secret of the nectar) had revealed his secret to Rama. Ravana called this the biggest mistake of his life.

   d. *Lessons for a King*: Ravana gave Lakshmana the following lessons about politics and statesmanship:
- Do not make an enemy of your charioteer, gatekeeper, cook and brother, they can harm you anytime.
- Do not assume you are a winner even if you are winning all the time.
- Always trust a minister or a colleague who criticizes you.
- Never assume your enemy is small or powerless as he had thought of Hanuman.
- Never assume that you can outsmart the Gods. You will always get what is present in your destiny.
- Do good without any procrastination or delay.
- Suppress greed as soon as you become aware of it.

Consult, Empower and Delegate

Clarity of what we want to achieve is important for any team. Rama was clear that he had to reach Lanka, defeat the evil Ravana and bring Sita back. This vision was shared with the entire team as soon as it was visualized. Rama also delegated responsibilities to various members of the team starting with the leaders Hanuman, Sugriva and Jambavanta.

Vibhishana disclosed Ravana's secret to Rama, which led to the end of the war. Rama vowed to protect Vibhishana. Several of the leaders of the army advised him not to trust Vibhishana but Rama convinced them of the goodness of Vibhishana.

Rama empowered his subordinates.

Pick the right team and trust them

Rama had to find a team of warriors for the forthcoming battle. Against an army of demons of Ravana who had defeated armies in all three worlds, Rama led a team of unlikely warriors. He instilled confidence in them and gained their trust.

While there were a lot of ideas on how to cross the sea, Rama took three days to meditate in order to decide what needed to be done. He picked Nala and Nila to complete the task. They were the engineers who constructed Rama Setu between India and Lanka so that Rama's army could cross over. Nala was the son of Vishvakarma, the presiding deity of all engineers, architects, builders, carpenters and craftsmen. To this day, Vishvakarma Puja is performed before Diwali to pray to instruments. Nila was the son of Agni and one of the leaders of Rama's Army.

Leaders must trust their teams if they want their vision to be achieved. It is also important to create an environment where new leaders are nurtured and given an opportunity to develop and grow.

Treat everyone equally

Rama did not see any differences in the social strata of people or their backgrounds. He treated everyone—people and animals—with the same level of respect, and this resulted in people going out of their way for Rama.

The story of Guha, a Nishada leader, is well known. Guha, a close friend of Rama, ferried Rama, Sita and Lakshmana across the Ganges River. Rama does not allow Guha to touch his feet because Rama thinks of Guha as his friend. Before they climb into the boat, Guha says, 'I heard the story of the stone turning into a woman (Ahalya) when your foot touched it. Now that you are getting into my boat, I do not want my boat turning into a woman when you get into it. So let me clean your feet before getting into the boat.' His purpose of touching the feet of his Lord was thus achieved.

Avoid judging anyone and develop a code of ethics

Rama is respected for his moral code and yet, he is not shown as a person who blindly follows his moral code and expects others to do the same. He chose not to judge anyone. Rama also believed that an unarmed individual must not be attacked.

When teams see a leader as being non-judgemental and focusing only on their work, their commitment levels are much higher.

Succession planning is important

Dasharatha had planned to hand over the kingdom to Rama. He had not thought of any challenges that could come in the way. Kaikeyi's demand for the two boons promised to her created an issue in the succession and resulted in the death of Dasharatha, leaving the throne without a ruler for 14 years.

Rama, when he was planning his succession, divided his kingdom equally among his sons Lava and Kusha.

A good leader must groom their team members and prepare them for any eventual succession. As the old saying goes, if you want to grow rapidly in your own job, develop a successor better than yourself and make yourself redundant in that role. Of course, it must be remembered that succession planning is generally successful if the leader is secure.

What Not to Do

Some lessons in the *Ramayana* also detail what not to do, which are as follows:

1. Never commit without understanding the full implications

Dasharatha was happy with Kaikeyi for saving his life in a battle and gave her two boons. When it was time for the coronation of Rama, Kaikeyi (influenced by her maid Manthara) decided to ask for these two boons so that her son Bharata would be placed on the throne of the Kingdom. She asked Dasharatha to make Bharata the Crown Prince and banish Rama for 14 years, to which Dasharatha had to agree. The result was not what Kaikeyi expected. Bharata refused the throne and instead chastised his mother. Rama, Sita and Lakshmana went into exile (into the forest) and King Dasharatha passed away.

The lessons are not to promise anything without understanding the complete implications and taking into account its ramifications.

2. Negotiate from a position of strength

Rama sent Angada as his emissary to Ravana seeking Sita's peaceful return. Ravana, driven by his ego that made him believe he was infallible, refused. Next, Hanuman met Ravana after burning Lanka, and once again offered the same. Ravana, without recognizing the power of Rama, spurned this offer as well.

The lesson we can take away is that a leader needs to evaluate the opposition after taking into account the relative strength of the leader's organization. Businesses could prosper or die because the leader, caught in his ego and a false sense of security, did not take corrective action on time.

3. Keep wise counsel

Kaikeyi had Manthara who clouded her mind against Rama. Ravana's wife Mandodari and his brother Vibhishana advised him several times to return Sita with full respect to Rama. Ravana was not willing to listen to their advice, suffering the consequences of his actions.

The lesson is to surround ourselves with a team of individuals who will give the correct advice instead of flattering you and simply accepting whatever you may say as you're their leader.

4. Do not covet what does not belong to you

There are so many stories in the *Ramayana* where greed was the cause of grief and problems. Kaikeyi wanted the throne for her son, which resulted in so many challenges for her family. Shurpanakha wanted Lakshmana to marry her. Lakshmana cut off Shurpanakha's nose and that led her to complain about it to her brother Ravana. Bali abducted the wife of his brother Sugriva, which led to Rama killing Bali and restoring the Kingdom to Sugriva. Ravana wanted Sita and ended up losing his Kingdom and his life.

The lesson is to do business ethically. Do not try to bypass laws or do things to secure a quick win. 'Get rich quick' plans seldom work!

5. Select your partners carefully

Rama needed a strong partner as he was building an army to reach Lanka. Bali was the stronger brother who had defeated

Ravana, but Rama chose Sugriva as his partner and then supported him in killing Bali and recovering the Kingdom of Kishkindha that rightfully belonged to Sugriva.

Our lesson is that we may partner with the wrong and unethical people for a short-term victory. However, in the long run, it will only hurt us and damage our reputation.

PERSONAL LESSONS

Lord Rama, the seventh avatar of Vishnu, is an example of chivalry and virtue.

In the words of Swami Vivekananda, Lord Rama is, 'the embodiment of truth, of morality, the ideal son, the ideal husband and above all, the ideal king.'

Several personal and life lessons that we can learn from his life and persona are as follows:

1. *Family is important, respect elders and bond with siblings*: From Rama accepting the wishes of his father to live in the forest for 14 years to Lakshmana following his older brother into the forest to Bharata deciding to place his brother Rama's slippers on the throne as the rightful heir, respect for elders can be observed several times in the *Ramayana*.

    Rama kept his father's promise. His father's honour became his own honour. He forgave his stepmother Kaikeyi for his banishment. Family bonds are important for each one of us.

2. *All that glitters is not gold and beware of temptations.* During exile, Rama, Sita and Lakshmana were living a peaceful existence, in harmony with nature, in the

jungle. Sita was enticed by the golden deer Mareecha, a demon who took the form of the deer, and sent Rama to catch him for her. When Rama did not return, Sita sent Lakshmana to bring him back. This was the moment that Ravana was waiting for and abducted Sita.

The lesson we can draw is not to run after sudden attractions. We need to value what we have instead of leaping towards the unknown and into the abyss.

The other lesson we can draw from this story is that we must follow instructions and not make decisions based on emotion. Had Sita followed Rama's instructions, the result may have been different!

3. *Never consider anyone inferior.* Rama ate fruit from the hands of poor Shabari who tasted each fruit first to ensure that the fruits she gave Lord Rama were tasty and sweet.

   Rama and Lakshmana also gathered an army of monkeys and bears, with Hanuman, Sugriva and Jambavanta in the lead.

4. *Remain humble.* When Hanuman met Sita in the Ashok Vatika, he could easily have taken her back. However, Sita turned down the offer and insisted that Rama would need to come and take her back. Hanuman also surrendered to Ravana and his army after burning Lanka where he, respectfully, asked Ravana to return Sita to Rama.

5. *Respect everyone because everyone matters.* Rama Setu, the bridge between the southernmost tip of India and the northern tip of Lanka was built entirely by monkeys and bears without almost any human interaction. Legend has it that a small squirrel also contributed to building the bridge. She carried pebbles on her back to contribute to the building process. Rama is said to have been so

impressed with the squirrel that he stroked her back with his hands, giving her the stripes on her back.

LESSONS FROM SITA

Sita is revered as the wife of Rama and as a Goddess. However, she never received the attention she deserves. There are a lot of lessons we can learn from her, both when she was with Rama in the jungle and as a captive of Ravana in Lanka as well as her life after she returned from Lanka and had to live in the jungle again, instead of the palace with Rama, which should have been her natural place.

Sita followed her conscience. When Ravana came to ask her for alms, she listened to her own voice, disregarding the instructions to stay within the *Lakshmana rekha* for her security. She believed that it was morally wrong to not provide alms to a hungry sadhu who had come to her home.

When asked to go through the *agni pariksha,* she did the needful as all the Gods watched. She walked through the fire, unscathed.

Sita brought up her sons Lava and Kusha on her own in the jungle, instilling the best values in her sons. When Lava and Kusha returned to the palace to tell Rama that they were his sons, Sita was called back but was faced with the same condition of an *agni pariksha*. She chose not to go ahead with this test again and instead asked Mother Earth to take her back.

LESSONS FROM LAKSHMANA AND BHARATA

1. Selfless brotherly love is very rare in today's world. Lakshmana worshipped his older brother Rama selflessly

and chose to leave his family behind in Ayodhya while he followed his brother into the forest.

Lakshmana stood like a shield in front of Rama and became the person who was available to do anything for both Rama and Sita throughout the years they spent in the forest.

2. Bharata could have simply accepted the throne. He was offered the Kingdom on a platter as a consequence of his father Dashratha fulfilling a vow to his mother Kaikeyi. However, his sense of right and wrong did not permit him to do what most others would have done. Instead, upon learning that his mother Kaikeyi had unjustly managed to get Rama banished from Ayodhya, he immediately went into the forest to look for Rama and offered him his rightful position as the ruler of Ayodhya.

So great was his devotion to his brother and so strong was his desire to be fair and just, that when Rama refused to return to Ayodhya before completing his 14 years in exile, Bharata placed Rama's sandals on the throne and ruled Ayodhya in the name of Rama. He did this till Rama returned to regain his rightful position.

In conclusion, the basic teaching from the *Ramayana* is that no matter how powerful evil is, it will always be defeated by good.

Truth always wins, no matter how vicious or poisonous the lie.

The most well-told lie has a dark agenda behind it.

The win of good over evil is a universal reality.

ANCIENT WISDOM

कर्मण्येवाधिकारस्ते मा फलेषु कदाचन।
मा कर्मफलहेतुर्भूर्मा ते सङ्गोऽस्त्वकर्मणि।।

—*Bhagavad Gita, Chapter 2, Verse 47*

I would like to end with the most famous verse from the *Gita*.

All management lessons finally come to an end with the work we do and what we expect in return from our work. This verse signifies the importance of work in our lives. It states that we must always be ready to perform our prescribed duties but we should not care for the fruits of our actions. We should neither consider ourselves the cause of the results of the activities we perform nor be attached to inaction.

The words, the central teaching of karma yoga, offer a deep insight into the spirit of the work we do. The verse talks about four areas relating to our work.

1. You have the right to work. Do your duty.
2. You do not have the right to the results of your work.
3. Do not work exclusively in anticipation of the results of your work.
4. Do not give up work/action for any reason.

Action (karma) and its fruit (result) are akin to cause and effect, and most religions/their scriptures accept this. The following words are derived from the concepts in Hindu philosophy regarding dharma and adharma (unrighteousness).

> *Dharma leads to Punyam leads to Sukham*
> *Adharma leads to Papam leads to Dukham*

Dharma leads to Punyam leads to Sukham

- *Dharma*: This refers to righteous living or moral order. It's the ethical path that we are expected to follow in our lives. *Dharma* is considered essential for the stability and prosperity of society and the welfare of all beings.
- *Punyam*: When we follow the path of dharma, we accumulate *Punya* (merit). *Punya* is believed to bring about positive karma, which influences the quality and circumstances of our lives in a beneficial way.
- *Sukham*: The positive karma from accumulating *Punya* leads to *Sukha* (happiness or pleasure). *Sukha* is a state of lasting well-being and contentment.

Adharma leads to Papam which leads to Dukham

- *Adharma*: This refers to actions that are considered unethical or immoral. It is the opposite of *Dharma*, and it disrupts the moral and social order.
- *Papam*: Engaging in *adharma* leads to the accumulation of *paap* (sin or demerit), which brings about negative *karma*. This negative *karma* is believed to affect our lives adversely.

- *Dukham*: The negative *karma* from accumulating paap leads to *dukha* (sorrow or suffering). *Dukha* represents a state of unease, discomfort and dissatisfaction.

The doctrine of *karma* states that good action, ethically done, leads to merit, which leads to happiness. Conversely, *adharma*, unethically done, leads to *paap* or demerit, which leads to unhappiness.

DO YOUR DUTY

Krishna tells Arjuna that the result of our work depends on our efforts. In addition to our efforts, our destiny, past karma, the will of God, efforts of others, cumulative karma of others involved and the situation we are placed in are also factors that impact our work. Therefore, if the result is not as per our expectations, we can get stressed.

He further tells Arjuna to focus only on the work and not worry about the result. We know that if we do not focus on the result, we generally do a better job with greater satisfaction.

When people play golf, they are focused on the number of strokes as well as the number of strokes of their opponents. If they could merely focus on playing the shots to the best of their ability, they would find it much more enjoyable and would probably play a much better round.

YOU DO NOT HAVE THE RIGHT TO THE RESULTS OF YOUR WORK

To perform actions is an integral part of human nature. Having come into this world, we all have various duties determined by our family situation, social stature and occupation.

The results are meant to please God and our objective is to serve Him.

Krishna tells Arjuna not to think of himself as the one enjoying the fruits of his actions.

DO NOT WORK EXCLUSIVELY IN ANTICIPATION OF THE RESULTS OF YOUR WORK

Krishna asks Arjuna to give up the ego of the doer. Our senses, mind and intellect are inert; God energizes them with his power and puts them at our disposal. As a result, only with the help of the power we receive from him are we able to work.

By way of example, the tongs in the kitchen are inactive by themselves, but they get energized by someone's hand, and then they perform difficult tasks, such as lifting burning coal, etc. The tongs are not the doers of actions. If our hand did not energize the tongs, they would not be able to do anything.

Similarly, if God did not supply our body, mind and soul with the power to perform actions, we would not be able to do anything. Thus, we must give up the ego of doing, remembering that God is the only source of the power by which we perform all our actions.

DO NOT GIVE UP WORK/ACTION FOR ANY REASON

We need to work and not run away from our work, even if the work seems to be too burdensome or confusing at times.

Thus, all management lessons can ultimately be summarized in Verse 47 of Chapter 2 of the *Bhagavad Gita*:

कर्मण्येवाधिकारस्ते मा फलेषु कदाचन।
मा कर्मफलहेतुर्भूर्मा ते सङ्गोऽस्त्वकर्मणि।।

And as stated earlier, I would like to repeat the four parts of this verse that we must always remember, no matter what situation we face at work or our life:

1. You have the right to work. Do your duty.
2. You do not have the right to the results of your work.
3. Do not work exclusively in anticipation of the results of your work.
4. Do not give up work/action for any reason.

ACKNOWLEDGEMENTS

I express my heartfelt gratitude to Dibakar Ghosh, Editorial Director of Rupa Publications, whose constant source of ideas and motivation has been invaluable throughout our collaboration. I would also like to thank my editor, Shatarupa Dhar, for her meticulous and dedicated work on the manuscript.